'Knots are elusive

but very important

details

of the Angler's equipment'

W. A. Hunter — 1927

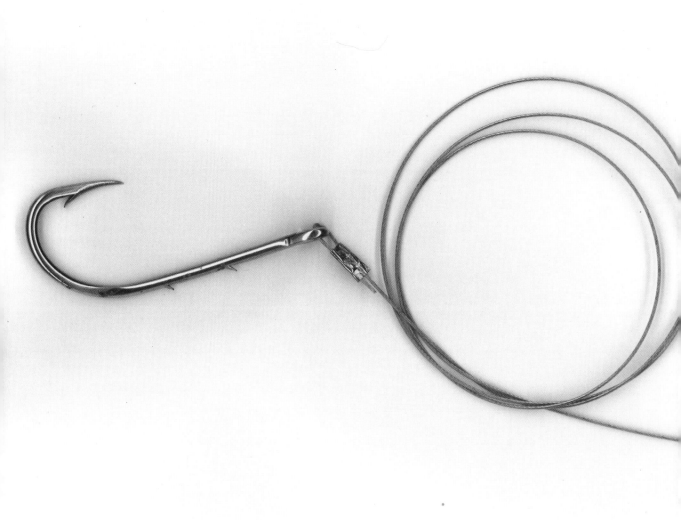

THE COMPLETE BOOK OF
FISHING
Knots

fundamental knots
loop knots
joining knots
hook, lure, swivel and sinker knots
other useful knots

Geoffrey Budworth

THE LYONS PRESS
Guilford, Connecticut
An imprint of The Globe Pequot Press

All inquiries should be addressed to:
The Globe Pequot Press, P.O. Box 480,
Guilford, Connecticut 06437

The Lyons Press is an imprint of The Globe Pequot Press

Library of Congress Cataloging-in-Publication data is
available on file

ISBN 1-55821-907-2

Executive Editor Mike Evans
Senior Editor Nina Sharman
Editor Caroline Bingham

Art Director Keith Martin
Executive Art Editor Mark Stevens
Designer Rozelle Bentheim
Production Joanna Walker

Illustration Line and Line

Picture acknowledgements

AKG, London/Erich Lessing 14 right
Corbis UK Ltd/Historical Picture Archive
15, /Gian Berto Vanni 14 bottom left
Mary Evans Picture Library 16 bottom
Octopus Publishing Group/Gary Latham 8-9

Typeset in Adobe Myriad, Monotype Walbaum and
Monotype Grotesque
Produced by Toppan Printing Co Ltd
Printed in China

contents

the knots

DIRECTORY OF KNOTS

<6>

<7>

ACKNOWLEDGMENTS

I am grateful to Dave Roberts of Medway Tackle in Tonbridge, Kent, for his professional advice and guidance freely given in the early stages of compiling this book, and especially indebted to fisherman Owen K. Nuttall[IGKT] of West Yorkshire*, for sharing with me so many of his original knotting ideas – not all concerned with angling – over the past 15 years. The cordage used to create specimen knots for the illustratations in this book came from a variety of sources, namely: English Braids Ltd., Malvern, Worcestershire; Footrope Knots, Ipswich, Suffolk; K.J.K. Ropeworks, Tiverton, Devon; Marlow Ropes Ltd., Hailsham, Sussex; and Oakhurst Quality Products Ltd., Edenbridge, Kent.

* The superscript designation IGKT is used throughout this book to indicate a member of the International Guild of Knot Tyers.

<8>

<9>

INTRODUCTION

The earliest Palaeolithic fishermen
used spears and harpoons ...
nets must have been invented
long after ... and, somewhere
between the two, primitive
man thought of catching fish
with a baited line.

Charles Chevenix Trench, 1974

The only bits of his or her fishing tackle that an angler
must still actually make are the knots; and, if these are
not to be the weak link in any rig, more consideration
must be given to them than to all of the other items
of shop or store bought accessories. Indeed, the time-
honoured good-luck wish from one angler to another,
expressed in the words 'tight lines and no breaks'
ought to be amended to 'tight lines and firm knots'
– except that leaving them to luck is not enough; knots
must be patiently learnt, diligently practised and then
used shrewdly.

Fishing knots occupy a narrow and specialized
niche in the wider knotting scene. They are a lot like
those used for mountaineering and caving; in fact
some of the knots are identical, the only difference
being the size and type of material in which they are
tied. Anglers' monofilament lines, braids, wires and
cables have diameters fifty times thinner than climbing
ropes and breaking strengths measured in kilograms
(or pounds) rather than tonnes (or tons). The lives of
mountaineers, cavers, surveyors, and assault and rescue

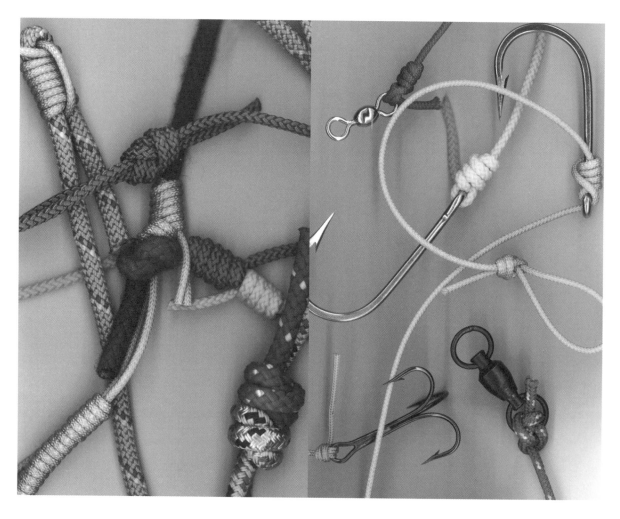

<10>

teams literally hang upon their knots; while the capture of elusive prey and trophy or prize-winning fish depends upon every knot an angler chooses to tie. These knots have emerged and evolved as solutions to problems in the utilisation of rope, smaller cordage and fine lines, so it may merely have been a similarity of need that led to similar knots.

Most anglers use very few knots, sensibly keeping to those they have found easy to tie as long as such knots keep the hook on the line, and that hook catches bait and fish. Knots are just like other tackle, however, in one respect. While it is possible to start out with just a few bits and pieces, it is desirable to collect over time a wider range of paraphernalia, so as always to have precisely the right thing for the job in hand. Unlike other accessories, however, knots can be acquired for little or no cash outlay, and carried in an angler's head (taking up no space and weighing nothing) so that one may learn as many as one likes.

<11>

HISTORY

Anglers take pride in having been among the earliest prehistoric contributors to the growth of the universal art, craft and science of knotting. There are now thousands of knots (and an almost infinite number of variations of some of them), ranging from boating bends and hitches to the macramé of handicraft practitioners and the cut-and-restored magic ropework of stage magicians; but the first useful knots were surely for snares, nets and fishing. Some time after early humankind learnt to hunt, the idea occurred of spearing and harpooning fish. Centuries later, net-making began.

At some undetermined time between these two epochal events, however, gorges (short lengths of horn, shell, flint and bone, sharpened at both ends to wedge in the throats of palaeolithic fish caught on hand-lines) appeared, and from these evolved the later Stone Age hooks of flint. An ancient settlement and garbage dump (now under 3m (10ft) of water off the coast of Denmark) has yielded up to archaeologists a 10,000-year-old bone fishhook. A short length of sinew, gut or such-like is still attached to the bony shank of the hook by the knot known today as a clove hitch.

Below Egyptian carved stone with fishing scene, *c.*2494-2345 BC.

Above Fishermen with net and rod depicted on an Italian vase, *c.* 480 BC.

Between 1600 and 1200 BC, the Mycenaean people of Ancient Greece used hooks of bronze that were both barbed and eyed. They may also have invented fly-fishing. Queen Cleopatra of Egypt (c. 68-30 BC) was a keen and successful angler. But it was British fishermen and women in the 13th and 14th centuries who largely pioneered and developed the methods later copied by anglers beyond the English Channel in mainland Europe, as well as those across the Atlantic in North America and Canada. We know this through the writings of the 15th-century Lady Prioress of Sopwell, Dame Juliana Berners (or Barnes) and later 17th-century gentlemen who included Gervase Markham, Izaak Walton, Robert Venables and Robert Nobbes.

For a comparatively brief period of about 150 years, spanning the 18th and 19th centuries, complicated knots of the ropeworking kind came to be associated with deep-water sailors. Today, however, it is climbers, cavers and especially anglers who tie elaborate knots, adding to the known knotting repertoire by discovering and naming many new ones.

<14>

MATERIALS

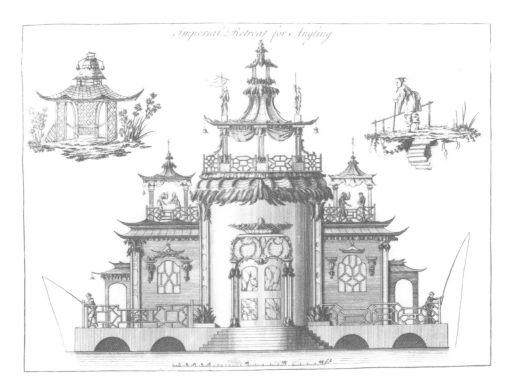

EARLY NATURAL MATERIALS

Humankind was probably tying knots 300,000 years ago in fibrous vines, as well as in the sinews and rawhide strips from animal carcasses, and we know, from artefacts dug up by archaeologists, that neolithic folk 10,000 years ago tied knots for nets and fishing lines. The Greek writer Plutarch (AD c. 46-120) recommended the hair from a thoroughbred white stallion's tail for fishing lines, his theory being that mares weakened their tails with frequent splashes of urine. He was wrong. It is more likely that coarse-bred animals (whether stallions, mares or geldings) have the tougher tails. But he was right when he advised the use of as few knots as possible in the making of horsehair lines because they might deter fish (he was the first person to record an awareness that fish reacted adversely to this sort of visual clue).

Dame Juliana, Prioress of Sopwell, was expert at all field sports but preferred angling above the rest. She made her own horsehair lines with no mean skill, knotting each 1m (3ft 3in) length to the next with a water knot or duchy knot, and then neatly binding the ends with fine silk thread. Her horsehair leaders ranged

Above This illustration depicts a peaceful Chinese fishing scene: the Imperial Retreat for Angling.

in thickness from one hair (for minnows) and two (for roach) up to 15 (for salmon); and each was bound and seized to the shank of its hook with silk thread, the spare working end of the leader turned back over this initial whipping, to be seized a second time atop the first binding layer. She then dyed her lines to echo water weeds: green (in summer), yellow and brown (in autumn), and tawney (in winter and early spring).

In 1682, Thomas Nobbes observed lines in use of mixed horsehair and silk, and even a few of silk and silver wire.

In the early part of the 1800s some British fishermen were still using horsehair lines (and believing Plutarch's notion that the tails of thoroughbred white stallions were best). Although in theory it ought to have been possible to spin horsehair lines in the same way as twine or string, they continued to be knotted, even though the knots tended to catch in the rod rings and impede the free running of reels.

Certainly horsehair was pleasant stuff to handle; supple yet not prone to bad snarls or tangles. The notable Victorian angler Francis Francis rated as his greatest achievement the landing of a 3kg (6¾lb) barbel, foul-hooked by its dorsal fin (its power and mobility therefore largely unimpaired), after three and a half hours on a single horsehair.

Late 19th-century undressed silk was prone to tangle. But, heavily oiled or greased, it could be tamed sufficiently to be cast into the wind, when it would also float. Twisted silk threads had been known in China since the 6th century; they are referred to even earlier in a 2,000-year-old legend concerning the Chinese Emperor Wu who, allegedly, fished with a white silk line attached to a golden hook baited with a goldfish. By contrast the Japanese Empress Zinga (AD 170-269), a model of frugality, is said to have caught a trout on a bent pin baited with grains of rice, on a line made from threads pulled from her garment.

By the 1900s lines of cotton, flax, so-called Indian grass (probably jute), silk and Japanese silkworm gut were the regular alternatives. Cat gut (obtained from several creatures – but never cats), for stringing musical instruments, was being used in Europe by the mid-17th century, although it too – along with silk – had been adopted by Chinese fishermen centuries before. Silkworm gut had also arrived in the West, to be followed in the middle of the 20th century by a gut

Above This 17th-century woodcut shows a fisherman with a rod and a line probably made out of horsehair or silk.

substitute. All these natural fibres had shortcomings. They were comparatively weak, allowed little abrasion before fraying, and were prey to mildew, rot, insects and vermin. Wet lines lost up to 15% strength and, when waterlogged, their weight increased. Soggy lines had to be painstakingly dried after every use. Still, they could be tied with comparatively simple knots.

SYNTHETIC (ARTIFICIAL) FILAMENTS

In the 1930s synthetic cordage was discovered and developed on laboratory benches in the test tubes and beakers of industrial research chemists. The most common synthetic materials are polyamide (nylon) and polyester (the best known trade names being Terylene and Dacron). There are two main grades of nylon. Nylon 66 was a product of the Du Pont laboratories and the first man-made fibre of merit available, while Nylon 6 (trade names Perlon and Enkalon) was subsequently developed by I.G. Farbenindustrie. Terylene was a British development from investigations at the Calico Printers Association, the sole rights of which were then acquired by I.C.I. During the Second World War, when other materials were in short supply, anglers began to try out these newcomers. Greater breaking strengths, weight-for-weight, meant that much thinner and lighter lines could be used than before, enabling more to be wound onto every reel. The big problem was that previously reliable knots proved insecure with the revolutionary monofilaments, which were as supple as silk but even more slippery. Knots tied in them frequently failed. So more elaborate ones had to be devised to cope with the new-fangled synthetics.

Synthetic monofilaments have breaking strengths that range from a mere 0.2kg (8oz) to a massive 45kg (100lbs) or more. Typical thicknesses – too small to be measured with an ordinary school 30cm (12in) rule – range from 0.08mm (³⁄₁₀₀₀in) for a 0.5kg (1 lb) line to 0.7mm (¹⁄₃₂in) for a 23kg (50lb line). Nowadays the discerning angler can buy lines that float, or others that sink, while some have more or less neutral buoyancy but can be made, in expert hands, to float or sink. Even different sinking rates are in-built; for

<16>

example, fly lines are made that sink slightly faster at the front than at the back, helping to place the fly in the target area. A range of colours renders these modern lines either highly visible, virtually invisible or nicely in-between. At least one make incorporates a colour change every 9.1m (10yd) for accurate depth control. Monofilaments are usually round in cross-section and of uniform diameter throughout their length; but specially extruded nylon casts or leaders may taper from – say – 0.8mm ($^5/_8$in) with a breaking strength of 29.5kg (65lb) down to something like 0.36mm ($^5/_{16}$in) with a 2.7kg (16lb) breaking strength.

NYLON MONOFILAMENT

The commonest material anglers have to tie is nylon monofilament. It is the strongest man-made fibre and is said to lack 'memory' (that is, it tends not to retain a previously imposed coil or curve). It has a specific gravity greater than that of water and so does not float. Nylon also has considerable natural elasticity, stretching under load up to 30% of the unloaded line length. This enables it to absorb sudden large shock-loading. An unwanted side-effect is that nylon wound back under strain onto a reel (especially one with a multiplier), as when retrieving a large and heavy fish, will be abnormally tight. Line in this condition should be re-wound without stretch onto another reel at the earliest opportunity. Nylon does absorb water, decreasing its breaking strength by as much as 10%, but it can be repeatedly stored wet without detriment, and will regain its original strength as it dries. Intrinsically hard-wearing, it nevertheless deteriorates with age. Smaller diameters may need to be replaced after just a season of use. Broken monofilaments can be rejoined with knots that will not snag in the tip ring. Nylon has a fairly high melting point of up to 260°C (500°F) and so has a reduced risk of melting due to friction; but it will, like other synthetics, be irremediably weakened at a much lower temperature than its melting point, and so it should not be brought close to the flames of items such as camping stoves or glowing cigarette ends. Nylon withstands attack from alkalis, oils and organic

Above (clockwise from top) Dark copper coloured monofilament, sold as 'the line fish can't see'; white Dacron™ (polyester) backing line; clear nylon monofilament.

solvents, but keep it away from car battery acid. It has excellent resistance to abrasion and to degradation from the ultraviolet radiation of sunlight.

BRAID POLYESTER (TERYLENE, DACRON)

Polyester has three-quarters the strength of nylon (but it is equally strong, wet or dry). It has far less stretch than nylon (5% as opposed to 30%) and pre-stretching during manufacture can remove most of the latent elasticity it does possess. It resists acids (alkalis to a lesser extent), oils and organic solvents. Like nylon it does not float and has about the same melting point and resistance to sunlight. Fishing braids of polyester are size-for-size three or four times stronger than the monofilament equivalents. This greater diameter can be a noticeable handicap in strong tidal flows, while re-tying broken braids results in knots that may jam at a tip ring or in the rod guides. Although polyester resists abrasion better than nylon and so lasts longer, the construction of braided lines renders them more liable to fray, and the final 3m (10ft) may have to be cut away periodically. Strong, reliable and hardwearing, but soft and pliable, it used to be that polyester knots were unlikely to slip or come undone. Some new power

<17>

braids are noticeably smoother and slicker, however, with a considerable reduction of up to 25% in knot strength. Such braids also have a tendency, in taut lines, to pull down (like a warm knife cutting into butter) through the reserve wound onto the reel spool – unless it has previously been very tightly wound.

KEVLAR

Kevlar is an organic polymer, immune to moisture and rot, which was discovered by Du Pont as long ago as 1965. Then there is Spectra or HMPE, the brand name of Allied Chemicals who manufacture this super-lightweight polyethelene (marketed by others as Dyneema and Admiral 2000). All of these so-called 'miracle fibres' have phenomenal strength (greater than an equivalent strand of stainless steel) and represent the costly cutting edge of fibre technology.

WIRE OR CABLE

Main line wire fishing (apart from traces for conger and members of the shark family) seems to have been

Above (clockwise from top left) Braided white Dacron™ (polyester) flecked with green, for saltwater angling; brass wire, 18-gauge (1mm diameter); braided wire cable for sea angling (0.6mm diameter); orange nylon monofilament shock leader; clear nylon monofilament shock leader; nylon-coated steel wire for big-game fishing.

widely adopted only since the mid-1980s. High grade, stainless steel single strands of wire are replacing older, piano wire leaders. In a range of diameters (the larger the number, the thicker the wire and the greater the breaking strength), these are twice as strong as the equivalent diameters of nylon monofilament – although the wires must be coiled and uncoiled with care, otherwise they may kink and break. Some anglers prefer wire to be brightly coloured, others prefer it dull. Braided wire leaders, nylon-coated or plain, will not kink but can acquire a persistent bend. Comparatively massive, multi-strand aircraft cable has been adopted for the pursuit of deep-water big game sports fishing.

<18>

NEW KNOTS

The emergence of synthetic lines in the 1950s compelled their users to find new knots that would hold firm in materials that sometimes seemed almost untiable. The immediate response was to add extra wrapping turns and tucks to existing knots. As a consequence, there are now a great many cumbersome and unlovely angling knots, when a better strategy would perhaps have been an imaginative search for original and more elegant alternatives. That is why a number of comparatively new knots – unknown to most anglers – are featured in this book.

Anyone can take an extra turn or two around a familiar knot, add a different tuck here and there, then claim to have invented a fresh knot. Many do just this every year, but the fact that their creations cannot be found in existing knot literature is not a sufficient reason to add them to the repertoire. First, any new knot must survive two severe tests: 'So what?' and 'Who cares?' In other words, firstly, is the knot superior in some useful way to others that already do the same job? Secondly, even if it is, can it be effectively promoted so that those who might adopt and use it are persuaded to do so? Put like this, these two questions are not as harsh as they at first appear.

It is a misguided precept that if a knot works, then no matter how ugly, it is acceptable. Effective knots are usually good-looking knots. As a general guide, every knot should also be:

- distinctive and infallibly recognisable

- no more complicated than necessary

- easily learnt and tied

- readily untied (angling and parcel knots excepted)

- stable, strong and secure

Right (from top to bottom) Water knot, true lover's knot, seizing bend and linfit knot. The first two knots are centuries old, while the other two are recent innovations.

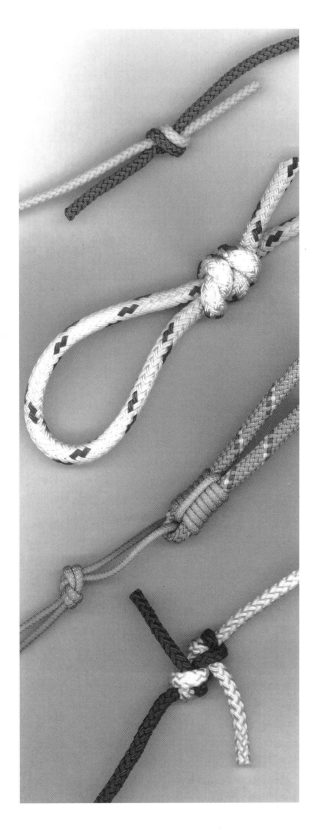

<19>

KNOT NAMES

Each plant, each butterfly, each
moth, each beetle, becomes
doubly real to you when you
know its name.

John Cowper Powys,
English novelist, 1872–1963

There is a consensus opinion within the International Guild of Knot Tyers that previously unknown or unrecorded knots – like the laws or rules and phenomena of more rigorous academic sciences – are not invented by their discoverers but merely identified and defined by them. The first individual to do so is quite justified in publishing a description of that knot, as a consequence of which his or her name may become forever linked with it. Some individuals actually patent knotted innovations – civil law recognizes a degree of ownership of knots – but it is merely the application (generally commerical) of the knot that is being registered and so protected in this way from exploitation by others.

Naming knots after individuals is viewed by the Guild with disfavour, primarily because it ignores and blurs the principles upon which more scholarly attempts at an overall knotting taxonomy (classification) are based. There is the added unspoken concern that those who name knots after themselves – or after whom knots are named by others – run the risk that such pride and presumption is very likely to be undermined, when research reveals that the knot pre-dates its latest re-discovery. Not infrequently, after one person has laid claim to a knot, someone else proves that it was already known and in use elsewhere at an earlier date. This does not wholly diminish the achievement of whoever genuinely recreates a little known or lost knot. Their efforts, after all, do serve to revitalize it. But a personal niche in knotting lore must be reserved for whoever found it first.

Anglers name their knots for esoteric reasons that make little or no sense at all away from the fishing scene. Some names describe a knot's function: blood loop dropper, sliding stop knot, spade end knot, arbor knot. Others hint, rightly or wrongly, at a place of origin: Bimini twist, Palomar knot, World's Fair knot, Australian plaited loop. A few indicate the method by which the knot is made – nail or tube knot, needle knot – or, alternatively, suggest its appearance: grinner knot, braided loop and splice. Some names are pretty: Alpine butterfly. Some are pretty nasty: strangle and hangman's knots. Still others display a hint of whimsy: true lover's knot, perfection loop.

In the 1950s, when books and booklets began to alert readers to nylon monofilament for fishing, just ten basic knots were recommended to cope with the new line. Since then a steady trickle of fishing knot books has promoted a 20-fold increase in the number of such knots. Taking into account all the mutations – accidental and deliberately induced – to these knots, as well as different methods of making some of them, there must now be at least 1,000 ways to tie a fishing line. Given the international appeal of fishing, it is inevitable that national and regional angling terms have arisen. But fishing knot names are – it must be said – in a mess. The same name may actually refer to different knots, and this has led to more than one instance of different written portrayals and descriptions for tying methods (even disparate anecdotes as to origins) for knots that turn out – when tied – to be identical. The 'offshore knot' is actually the cat's paw (a name in continuous use since the late 1790s. The basic fisherman's knot or bend became known to early 19th-century anglers as the water knot (confusing it with the other water knot). It has also been known as the waterman's knot, the angler's knot, the English knot, the Englishman's knot, the true lover's knot (one of many), and even the halibut knot. The double fisherman's knot is now the grinner knot, while the treble fisherman's knot has, by quirky arithmetic, become the double grinner (or paragum) knot. Of course, knots need names, but, as the late Desmond Mandeville[IGKT] ruefully concluded his poem about the importance of naming them:

... worse than those that have not any,
Some knots there be that have too many.

<20>

Modified knots are commonly re-named 'improved twisty-tucky knots' or 'perfected thingummy loops', while finger-flicking sleight-of-hand ways to tie them end up as separate index entries for a '20-second, fast' or 'speed nail knot' and the 'emergency dropper knot'. These superfluous adjectives only muddle matters more. Naming knots after eminent anglers and tackle makers, or the first person to tell an angling reporter about it, has already been discussed and discounted.

It must be hoped that the global spread of data now possible via electronic information technology – see just some of the thousands of entries listed under 'Knotting' on the Internet – will ultimately iron out such confusing anomalies, and not further muddy the waters of knotting nomenclature. Every effort has been made in this book to avoid contentious knot names. Simple labels – double overhand loop, one-way sheet bend, whipping – have been preferred. Others – such as the Palomar knot, Turle knot and water knot – reflect long established knotlore. A very few – the twined-&-twisted ligature knot is one, the torus knot is another – have been chosen in an effort to overcome other inconsistent references seen elsewhere.

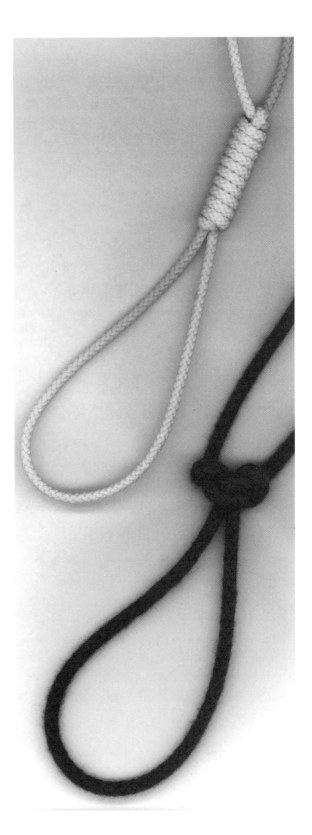

Right The knot at the top is known as a hangman's knot – a pretty nasty name, whereas the knot below is an Alpine butterfly – a very pretty name.

<21>

USEFUL TERMS

Knots tied in the comparatively tiny diameters of even the thickest fishing lines are referred to simply as knots. The nautical terms 'bends' and 'hitches', for joining knots and ring attachments respectively, are ignored by anglers. The end of a line used to tie knots is referred to as the working end or when it is inert the tag or tag end (by anglers). The other is the standing end. In between lies the standing part of the line. A doubled portion is a bight, until it crosses over itself when it becomes a loop, maybe with an extra half a twist to create an elbow (see fig. 1). Wrapping a line around a post or rail is called 'taking a turn' but bringing the working end around an extra half a turn creates a round turn (see fig 2).

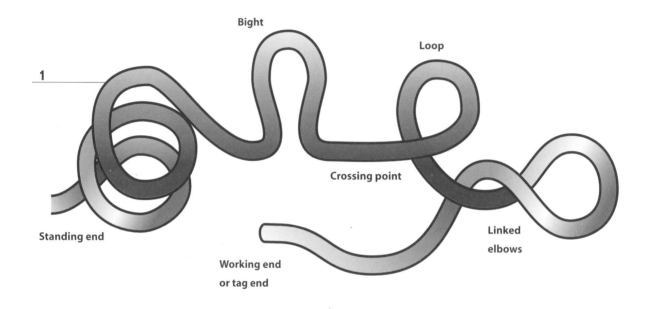

1

Bight

Loop

Crossing point

Standing end

Linked elbows

Working end or tag end

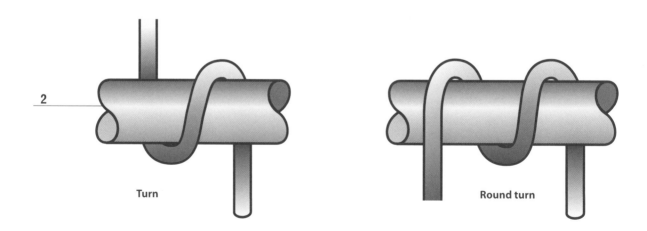

2

Turn

Round turn

<22>

KNOT STRENGTH AND SECURITY

An overhand knot more than halves the breaking strength of any line in which it appears, so it should never be allowed to remain in a fishing line with the vain hope that, once pulled tight, it will go unnoticed. It will quickly cause a loaded line to part; and, expressing the actual breaking strength of the knotted line as a percentage of its theoretical unknotted strength, the overhand knot is said to be 45-50% efficient. This makes it a weak knot. In contrast, any knot that safeguards the breaking strength of a line – such as the Bimini twist and the plaited loop (both of which, their adherents claim, leave lines as strong as if they were unknotted) – are rated 100% efficient. The bulky and barrel-shaped knots with lots of wrapping turns known as 'blood knots' are strong knots. Three or four wrapping turns are generally sufficient in heavy lines (23-45kg/50-100 lbs), while six or seven are needed for lighter lines (up to 4.5kg/10lbs), but add an extra four or five wrapping turns to those figures in the latest super-slick power braids. Most established fishing knots are 80% or more efficient but – while this is scarcely a matter of life or death (at least for the human holding the fishing rod) – it should be recognized that this rating still pares up to one fifth from the advertised breaking strength of the line. Nevertheless, over 80% represents a fairly strong knot.

We still do not know exactly how or why knots work. What little research has been done on the breaking strengths of individual knots ranges from outdoor observation and experienced guesswork, or rough-and-ready experimentation by anglers at home, to data generated from more controlled tests in the laboratories and factories of tackle makers. Published facts and figures vary between sources, however, seeming to depend upon the test rigs used by competing manufacturers, each of whom is (understandably) keen to out-do the opposition in the presentation of its products. It is therefore not possible to compare like with like. Book after book has for half a century listed the double overhand loop as 74% and the one-way sheet bend as 69% efficient, but these pedantic statistics are almost certainly average figures

gleaned from a range of outmoded test results; yet, without knowing precisely how the tests were conducted, any outcome is mostly meaningless. How those two knots actually perform from day to day will depend upon the material in which each knot is tied and what is then done to it. For instance, rate of load is a critical factor; a knotted line that can barely handle a given strain for 60 seconds will need to be more than twice as strong to cope with an identical load applied over half that time.

Most knots weaken the lines in which they are tied; and when one breaks, it is commonly observed that it does so at the knot. To learn how and why this is so would take a working party of scientists and engineers from several fields (physics, chemistry, mechanics and mathematics). No doubt stresses and strains occur when sharp bends are imposed upon any monofilament, but it can also be assumed that adjacent parts within a knot rub and may abrade (even cut) one another. It follows that each knot must be thought of as a potentially weak link; and the strength of a series of different knots will be that of the weakest one. Real life introduces variable factors that can make nonsense of controlled experiments. For this reason the statutory safe working load permitted by health and safety regulations for ropework or wire rigging upon which human lives depend – for example, a window cleaner's cradle or a ship's lifeboats – is as little as one seventh the manufacturer's estimated breaking strength of the rope or cable involved. Given all of these factors, the meaning of the statement in the glossy brochures of some suppliers that lines are rated in 'knotted breaking strengths' is far from clear.

KNOT SECURITY

Anglers require knots that can be relied upon to be both strong and secure – but strength and security are two different characteristics. Intermittent tugging or shock loading may cause some knots, which withstand large steady loads, to slip or capsize when they might not otherwise do so. Such knots may be strong but are less secure. Slippage can also affect knot strength, of

<23>

course, as internal knot parts rub against one another, generating melting heat or cutting abrasion. To test knot security, subject it to the repeated consistent dropping of a small weight, or simply tug on it by hand 100 times and count how many times the knot fails. An IGKT member who is a veterinary surgeon stitches trial suture knots into a car cleaning sponge and then subjects them to 15 minutes of turmoil in his washing machine, where they will be warm, wet, slimy and tugged spasmodically this way and that – exactly the conditions they must survive in living animal tissue. He only uses those that come out intact. Angling knots could be similarly tested, using cold water. John Smith[IGKT] tries out unknown knots in a short length of elastic (bungee) shock cord. Even tried-and-trusted

knots behave unpredictably (generally less well) in this curious cordage; but others, such as the angler's loop, perform well.

It has been estimated that a comprehensive review of fishing knots would fall into three discrete categories: knots to hooks, swivels, lures, etc. (65%); line-to-line joining knots (20%); and miscellaneous loops, stop knots, snoods, etc. (15%). In this book there are five knot sections, their contents carefully chosen and more evenly proportioned.

Below A Bimini twist safeguards the breaking strength of a line and, according to its supporters, leaves the line as strong as if it was unknotted, that is, 100% efficient.

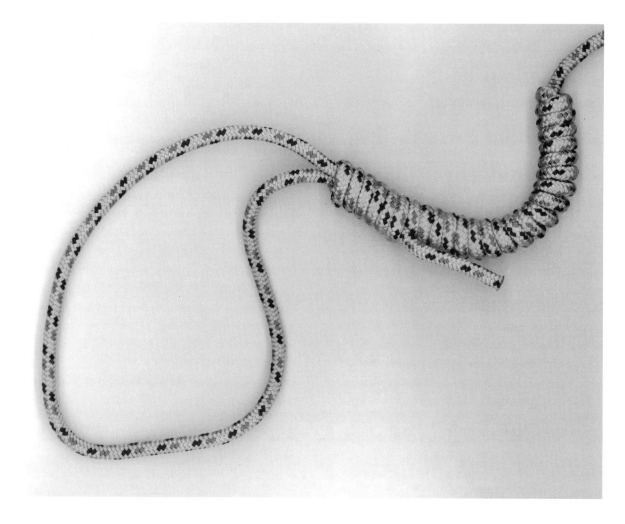

<24>

TYING KNOTS

There is only one correct way to tie any knot. Carelessly take the working end over where it should go under, or vice versa, and a different knot results – or, sometimes, no knot at all. The illustrations in this book allow no laxity or freedom of choice. Follow them meticulously, with this proviso; if you find tying the knot as it is illustrated and described does not come as easily or naturally to you as making its looking glass alternative, then feel free to tie it the other way round.

Fishing knots are best learnt for the first time indoors where conditions are warm, dry and comfortable. Use something larger than fishing line for early attempts to master these specialised knots; a length or two of flexible braided nylon, Terylene or polypropylene cord, each about 2m (6½ft) long and 5mm (¼in) in diameter, which can be bought from any DIY superstore or high street hardware shop, is ideal. Have one of each colour, so as to see exactly what happens when joining two lines together. Practise until the desired knots can be reliably done on a large scale every time. Most should take no more than a minute each to tie.

Tying fishing knots in fishing line is a little like model-making, requiring trained fingers, acute eyesight (whether natural or assisted), an appropriate working surface, good light, patience, inventiveness, and a few helpful tools. These tools include a sharp craft knife or scalpel, scissors, nail clippers or other end-cutting pliers. They may be domestic items, but angling suppliers can provide purpose-made ones. There are also a few high quality implements available through tackle shops, even if not routinely stocked, that actually aid in tying the surgeon's knot, the clinch knot, blood knots, nail and needle knots, the Bimini twist and haywire twists. They are excellent products. If machine-tooled metal gadgets and gizmos appeal to you, then ask your local supplier to track down and obtain one or more of them. Many self-sufficient anglers will, on the other hand, consider this extra cash outlay unjustified,

Right Self-sufficient anglers may occasionally use one foot or both feet to help them tie a particular knot.

<25>

preferring to improvise an occasional third hand with their lips and teeth, and occasionally one or both feet.

Knots should be dipped briefly into water, prior to pulling them tight, after which they draw up more easily and bed down more snugly. Knots lubricated this way tighten better and are more likely to realize their optimum strength. Without such treatment they may be up to 20% weaker. Some practitioners literally spit and polish knots, with anything handy that seems to do the trick, from saliva to proprietory brands of fluid dispenser or spray (for example, fish-attracting oil, or hand and lure cleanser), powered graphite, dry lube stick and silicone furniture polish. It is impossible to say, without knowing the chemical composition of such what other undesirable adverse long-term effects these products might have upon knotted lines. Water is probably best. Saliva should perhaps not be used, quite apart from reasons of hygiene, because it contains a digestive enzyme that could weaken knot and line.

For working knots in actual fishing lines, tie all you expect to use the day before setting out for the boat, beach, riverbank or reservoir. The TV presenter's constant refrain of '…here's one I made earlier' is invaluable for anglers too.

The completed knots illustrated in this book have longer ends than should be left in reality. Trim tag ends close to tight knots, cutting them at an angle of 45 degrees and leaving a short length protruding to allow for some slippage into the knot when it is loaded. This should be as little as 2mm ($^1/_{16}$in) for the lightest lines, 4mm ($^1/_8$in) for medium lines, and 7mm ($^1/_4$in) for heavy lines. After fighting a heavy fish, these safety

margins may have been reduced to half the original lengths. Do not burn tag ends with a lighted match, cigarette lighter or camping stove flame, since the heat can glaze and weaken the nearby knot and line.

Tightened knots may be rendered even more secure with a coating of nail polish, rubber-based cement or superglue, then further streamlined with plastic sleeves or a seizing of dental floss.

It is commonly stated that fishing knots should be pulled tight in one swift movement, but that is only true (in the case of blood knots and others which transform themselves) once the loose and newly-tied knot has assumed its finished layout; otherwise a mess more similar to a bird's nest can result. First remove all undesirable slack from the knot, at the same time kneading and shaping it with the fingers into more or less its final form. Then pull steadily on whatever ends or parts of the line will tighten the knot as required. Heavier lines cannot be fully tightened with unaided hands; use a glove or rag for extra purchase around the standing part and grip the tag end with of a pair of pliers; similarly protect the hands from cuts that lighter lines can inflict.

As with other types of knots, when an angling knot goes right, it seems easy. Even practised knot tyers, however, will make a botch of one now and again; and, once the tension and turns go awry, there may be no alternative but to cut it off and begin again, since badly tied knots drastically weaken line by as much as 50%. Often it is pointless to persist with an intractable knot. If at first you don't succeed – give up. In this context, it is not a bad maxim.

<26>

FIRST AID

The sole purpose of any fish hook is to impale and then resist removal; so, during the tying process, take great care not to prick or stab either hand. Many first aid manuals omit any mention of how to deal with a barbed hook beneath the skin, no doubt implying that any such injury should be treated only by qualified medical practitioners. If, however, such help cannot be obtained within a reasonable time, and self-help is vital for the continued well-being of the injured person, then the following tip comes from *The First Aid Manual* of the British Red Cross and St John Ambulance Brigade (6th edition, published by Dorling Kindersley, 1992).

1 Loop 1m (3ft) length of line around the hook (fig. 1).

2 Depress the eye end of the hook until it is flat on the skin. Also press down on the shaft of the hook so that, during withdrawal, the eye end of the hook will remain held downwards next to the skin. Tighten the line until all slack has been removed and it is just beginning to tug on the hook.

3 Pull sharply on the line, with good follow-through, so that the hook is removed via the point of entry.

Apply antiseptic first aid treatment to the wound and seek qualified medical aid as soon as possible, particularly in respect of the possible need for anti-tetanus treatment.

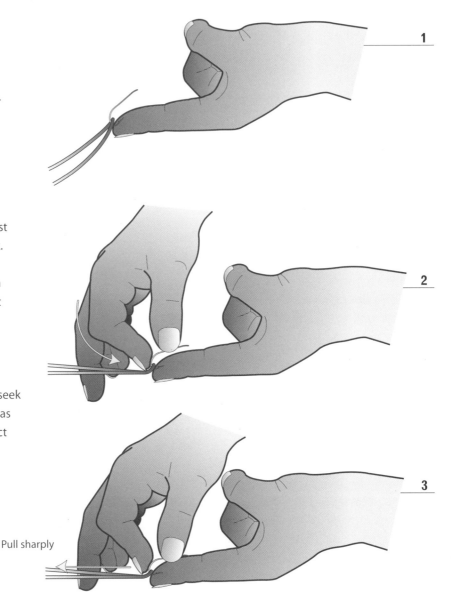

1

2

Pull sharply

3

<27>

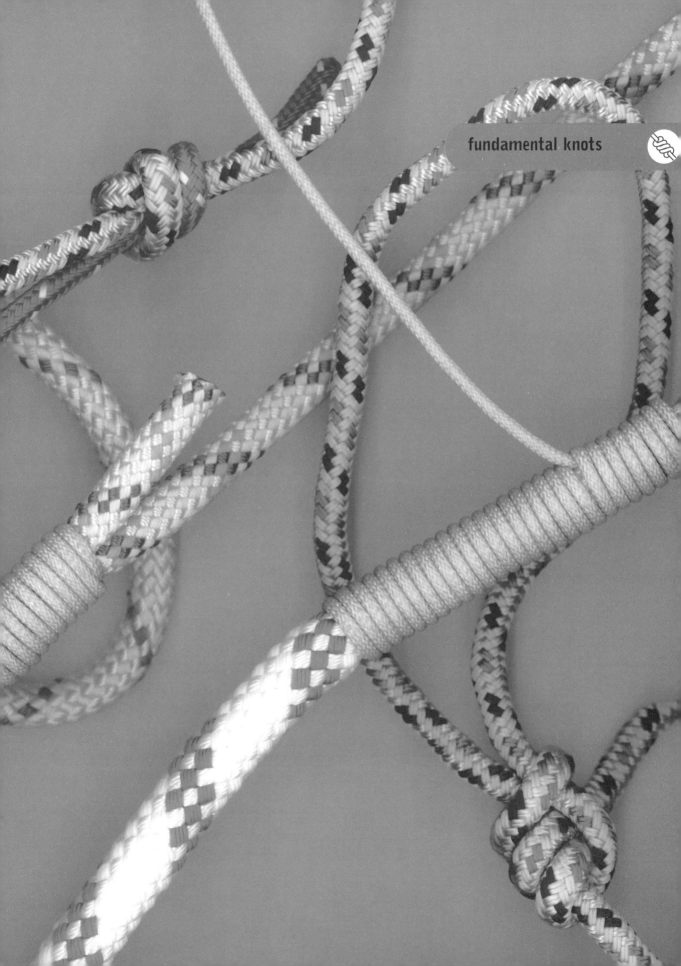

OVERHAND KNOT

APPLICATION

The simple overhand knot, which every child can do, is a knot nobody has to be taught to tie. It even ties itself in untended coils of line or airborne casts (which is why fly fishermen sometimes call it the wind – rhyming with 'sinned' – knot. Untie such accidental knots promptly as, once tight, they will break a loaded line.

METHOD

To tie an overhand knot, merely make a loop and pull the working end through it (figs. 1-2). There is a similar knot (fig. 3) with working and standing ends reversed. Both of these knots are classified as right-handed, because the two entwined knot parts spiral or helix to the right (that is, clockwise).

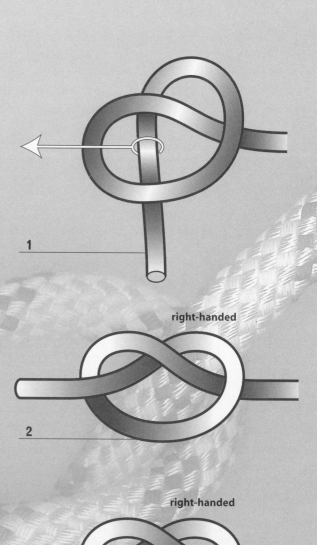

1

right-handed

2

right-handed

3

These most basic knots have mirror images (figs. 4-5, however, which are left-handed because the knot parts helix to the left (anti- or counter-clockwise). Be alert to knot handedness – which is nothing to do with whether the person tying it is right- or left-handed. At least two knots in this book (the twined-&-twisted ligature knot and the plaited interlocked loops) require the ability to identify and tie deliberate left- or right-handed spirals or helixes.

left-handed

4

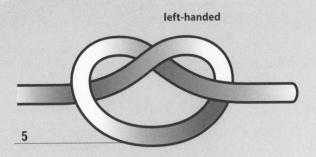

left-handed

5

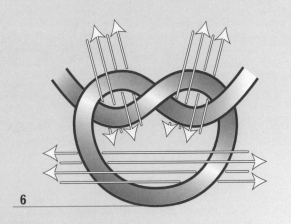

6

The overhand knot has three crossing points, where one knot part goes over or under another, creating a trio of distinct compartments or spaces that may be fancifully regarded as two eyes and a large mouth. Any further tuck made with an end of the same (or another) line through one or other of the two eyes can be made in any one of four different ways (fig. 6), depending upon the direction of tuck and whether the working end is led over-then-under or under-then-over. See how, in four out of the eight permutations

shown, the eyes remain separated; but, in the other four, the tucked line could slip unopposed from one into the other (and some angling knots take advantage of this characteristic whereby the entwined knot part is treated as having just one common opening).

Four alternatives are also possible in tucking through the open mouth (sometimes referred to as the belly) of the knot. This makes the overhand knot the basis for a variety of more elaborate knots with angling applications.

<31>

FISHERMAN'S KNOT

APPLICATIONS

A couple of sliding overhand knots can be used to join lines of the same diameter and material.

METHOD

Lay both lines parallel, tying an identical overhand knot with each working end to enclose the adjacent standing part, then tighten the knots until they are embedded together as shown (figs. 1-3).

HISTORY

This is a classic angling knot, centuries old, which – even tied in hempen hawsers aboard square-rigged sailing ships – was known as the fisherman's bend: "One day I was on the forecastle with Mr. Chucks, the boatswain…he taught me a fisherman's bend…and Mr. Simple," he continued, "there is a moral in that knot… the necessity of pulling together in this world…when we want to hold on." (from *Peter Simple* by Captain Frederick Marryat, 1834).

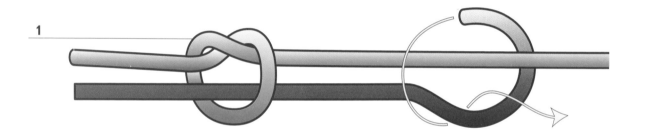

1

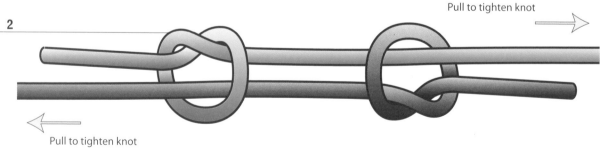

2

Pull to tighten knot

Pull to tighten knot

3

<32>

STRANGLE KNOT

METHOD

The strangle knot (fig. 1-3) is a more robust noose, its extra overlaid wrapping turn creating enough friction to trap the tag end and augment the breaking strength of this knot. The basis of this sliding loop is actually a double overhand knot.

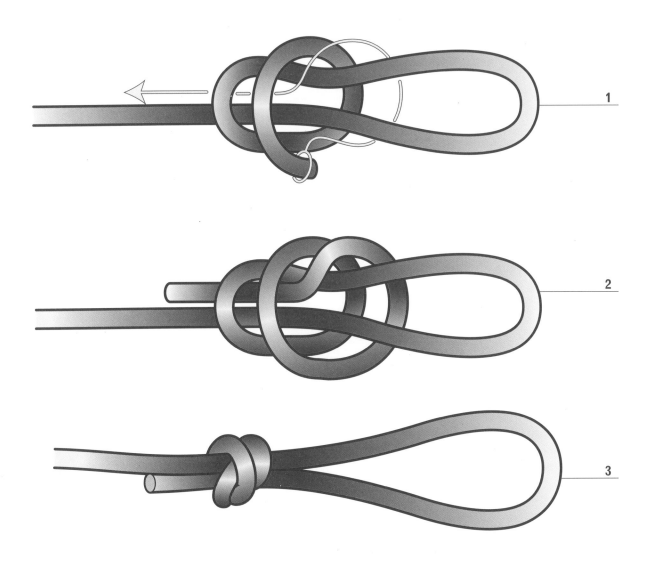

1

2

3

<33>

SLIP KNOTS

METHOD 1 (DIRECT)

If a longer working end is not pulled completely through the mouth of the overhand knot, but left as a protruding tongue (called a drawloop), then one or other of two possible slip knots is made (figs. 1-2 or 3-4). These are useless as loop knots, since any load placed upon them would promptly pull out the tag ends, unless they are secured by tying or crimping them to the standing part of the line to make fixed loops.

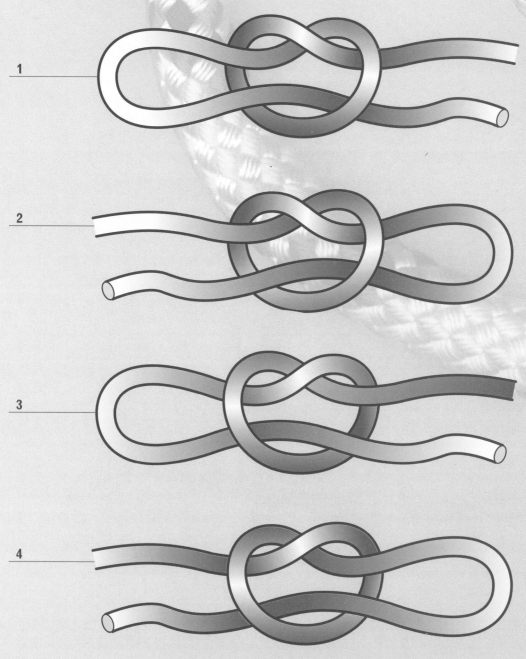

1

2

3

4

<34>

METHOD 2 (INDIRECT – ORTHODOX)

Several fishing knots – for example, the true lover's knot (known to some anglers as the Homer Rhodes knot) – begin with a slip knot attached to the ring of a hook, lure, sinker (weight) or swivel. This necessitates first tying an overhand knot, then passing the working end through the ring (and back in the same direction through the mouth or belly of the knot), to end up with an orthodox loop (figs. 1-2) that would otherwise be tied directly in the hand.

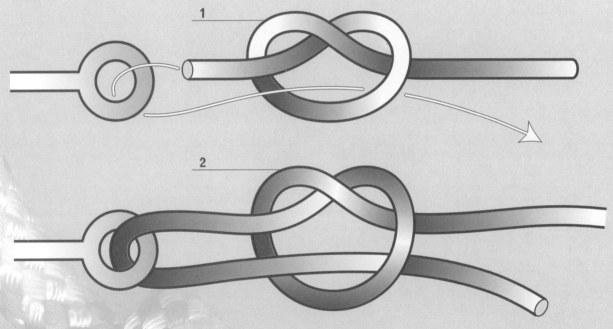

METHOD 2 (INDIRECT – SKEWED)

In bringing the working end back through the mouth or belly of the overhand knot, it is possible to re-enter it from the opposite direction to which the end emerged earlier; this results in a skewed slip knot, which is not often desirable, but at least one well-known attachment – the Rapala knot (see p. 50) – is tied this way.

<35>

FIXED LOOPS

METHOD 1

Tie a slip knot (fig. 1), then take a turn with the working
end around the standing part of the line and finally tuck
it through beside the initial knot (fig. 2). Work the entire
arrangement snug and tight (fig. 3).

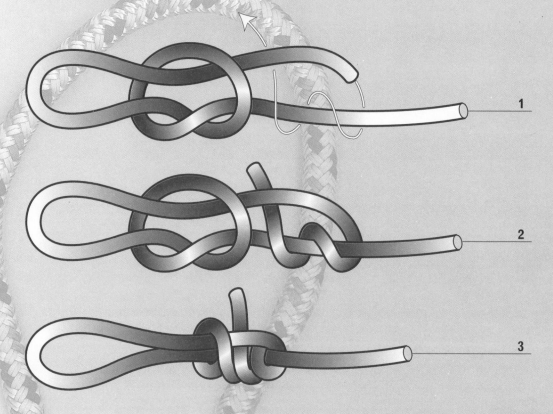

1

2

3

<36>

METHOD 2

The common compartment that exists between the two twined parts of an overhand knot is a particularly secure place to locate a tag end and this fixed loop knot exploits that feature. Tie a basic slip knot (fig. 1), then wrap the working end three or four times around the standing part (fig. 2) before tucking the tag end as shown (figs. 3-4). Tighten the knot, ensuring that the wrapping turns bed down snugly alongside one another and against the initial knot (fig. 5).

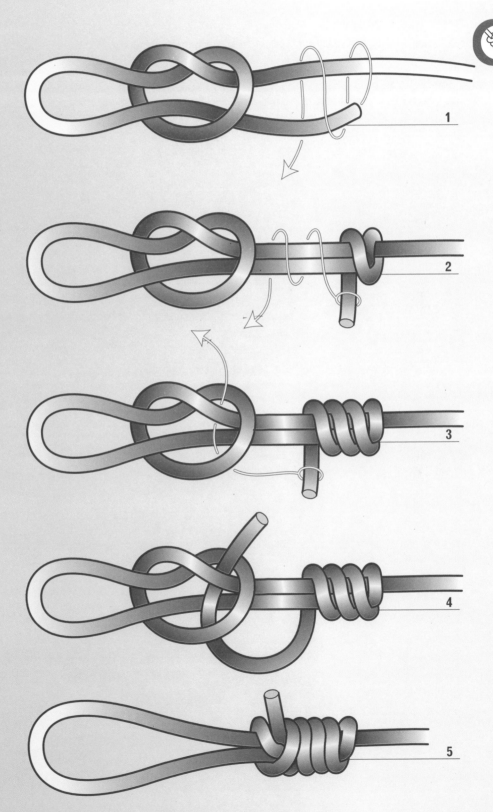

<37>

SIMPLE NOOSES

METHOD 1 (DIRECT)

Tie an overhand knot – this time working *away* from the tag end – and pull out a bight or drawloop in the standing part of the line (fig. 1) to make a basic right-handed, adjustable, sliding loop or noose. Once again, there is an optional left-handed mirror image (fig. 2), as well as an indirect tying method (fig. 3). These are quite unreliable as fishing knots, despite their five crossing points, but they are capable of being reinforced to serve as angling loop knots.

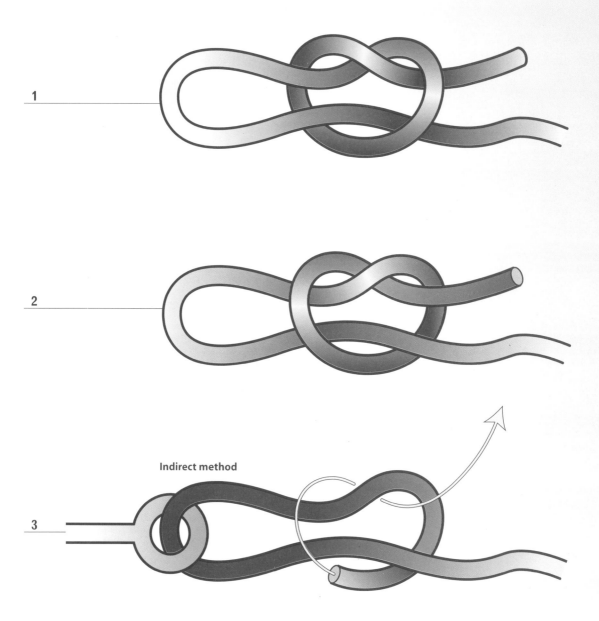

1

2

Indirect method

3

<38>

METHOD 2 (NOOSE INTO FIXED LOOP)

Any noose may be readily converted to a fixed loop by first tying an overhand knot in the adjustable loop (figs. 1-2) and then sliding the initial knot along until it jams against the added knot (fig. 3). In this example, the outcome is a true lover's knot (to be featured in the following section on Loops). This can be a time-saving short-cut to avoid cutting off one knot, then tying another – but realize that, if done in a more substantial noose knot, the new combination will be much weaker (only as strong as the overhand loop knot).

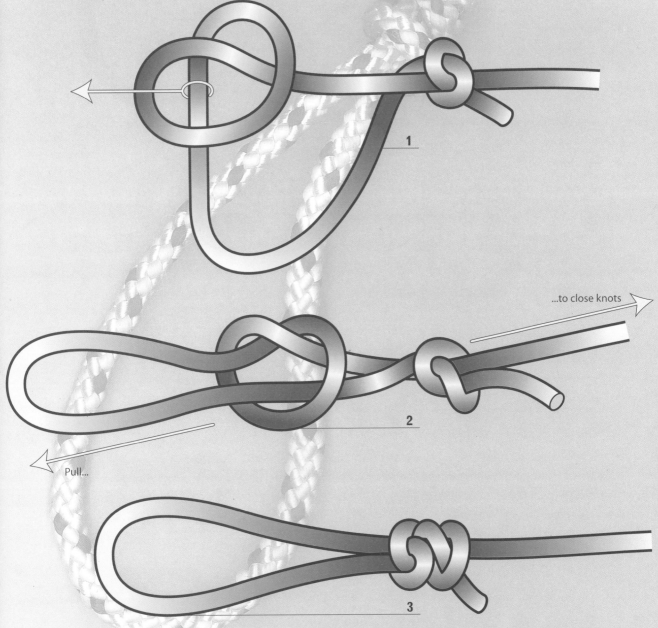

1

...to close knots

2

Pull...

3

<39>

BASIC BLOOD KNOT

METHOD

The preceding strangle knot is just the first and smallest in a series of multiple overhand knots, also known as blood knots (because – according to persuasive knotlore – either they are the basis for knots once used by surgeons in surgical ligatures and sutures, or because their addition to the lashes of a cat-o'-nine tails would draw blood). Tying these knots is an essential technique to be acquired by all anglers. Try one for the first time in a short length of flexible braided cord about 5mm (¹/₄in) in diameter. Make a simple overhand knot, then tuck the working end at least twice more (fig. 1). Start to pull both ends of the line apart. Feel the way the knot tends to twist. Go with it, rotating the ends of the line in opposite directions (as illustrated) so that the belly of the knot begins to wrap itself around the entwined knot parts (figs. 2-3).

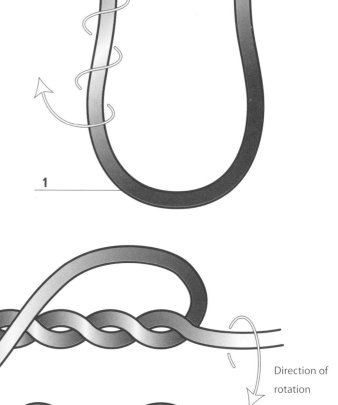

1

Direction of rotation

2

Direction of rotation

3

Ensure that the overlying turns are neat and snug, then pull the knot tight (figs. 4-5). Blood knots are used for several angling loop knots, for joining knots, and as knots to attach the hook, lure or swivel.

4

5

<40>

DEFORMED BLOOD KNOT

METHOD

Any inexpert or uneven pull upon a multiple overhand knot (fig. 1) results in a bastardised form of blood knot with wrapping turns unresolved and contained within a characteristic overlaid diagonal knot part (fig. 2). Opinion is divided over whether or not such a capsized version of the true knot merits separate consideration, but the fact is that some anglers are in the habit of tying and incorporating them into various fishing knots, calling them universal (or uni) knots and loops. This branch of the blood knot family may have mutated from book illustrations that failed to make clear how the essential transformation from initial multiple overhand knot configuration into final barrel-shape is achieved. They are probably best avoided, unless the material being tied is truly intractable, since the exposed diagonal knot part is very vulnerable to snagging underwater obstacles and sustaining abrasive nicks and cuts; and, if it breaks, the entire knot will unravel.

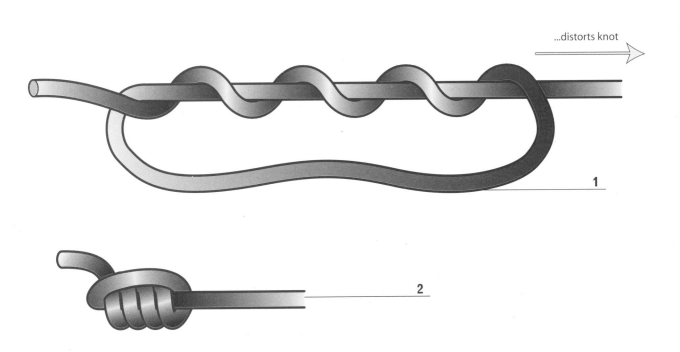

...distorts knot

1

2

<41>

WHIPPING

APPLICATION

Whipping is the generic name for any tight binding, whether it is used on a larger scale to prevent the cut ends of boat ropes from fraying, or forms the solution to a fishing tackle requirement. It is the basis for several fishing knots or loops. Depending upon how they are tied, as well as the use to which they are then put, various names are applied to them (nail knot, needle knot, tube knot or snelling) but the result is more or less the same in each case.

METHOD 1

Lay a length of line along the foundation around which the knot is to be tied, together with a narrow tube (a drinking straw or the hollow carcase of a ballpoint pen), and begin to bind the working end tightly around as shown (fig. 1). Continue this binding until at least six or seven turns have been completed (fig. 2). Then tuck the working end through the tube (fig. 3) and withdraw it so that the working end emerges from the opposite end of the binding to the standing end (fig. 4). Pull on both tag ends to tighten this knot and then trim them close to it (fig. 5). Because of the way it is tied, this is known as the tube knot. As an alternative to a tube a nail can be used, although this only makes a space through which the working end must then be tucked alongside, in which case it is referred to as a nail knot.

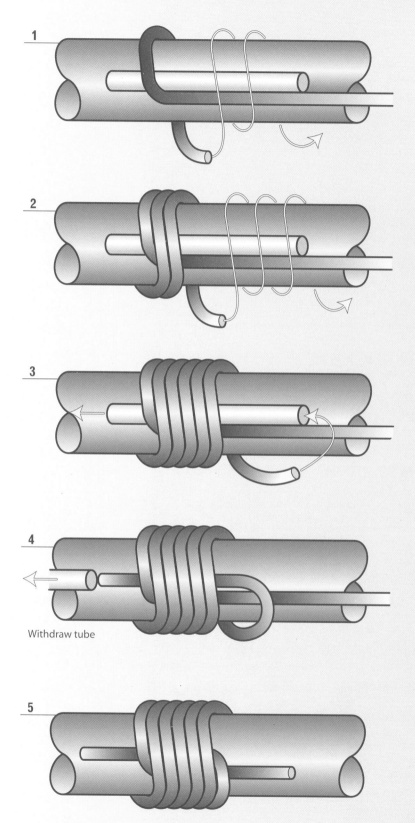

Withdraw tube

<42>

A needle or bodkin may be used instead (but do not call the result a needle knot – that is something else and will be featured in the section on Other Useful Knots), or you could use a long bight of separate line. But the tube is often preferable, since it permits the working end to be tucked without disturbing the wrapping turns, whereas a needle, bodkin or bight of line must drag the threaded – and thus doubled – working end through the untightened knot, and there is every chance of snagging and upsetting it.

Tie this knot loosely, in practice, to discover how the two ends should be interlinked, so that when the binding is tightened they become half-knotted together (fig. 6). The friction of these entwined knot parts, overlaid by the tight binding turns, combine to make this an intrinsically neat and fairly secure arrangement that can then be rendered semi-permanent with a coating of superglue or such-like.

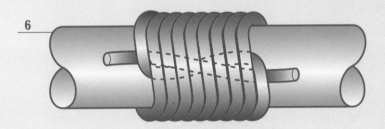

6

A pair of nail knots about 7mm (¼in) apart will convert a bight of line into a fixed loop (fig. 7). Use light monofilament which will bite into any surface coating on the loop line. Coat both knots with a rubber-based cement or other glue.

A pair of nail knots

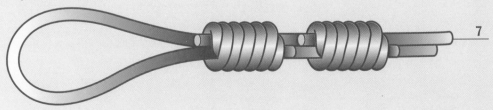

7

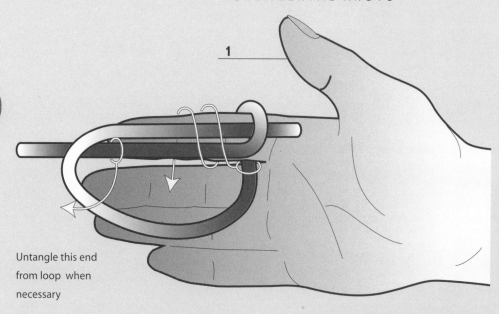

1

Untangle this end
from loop when
necessary

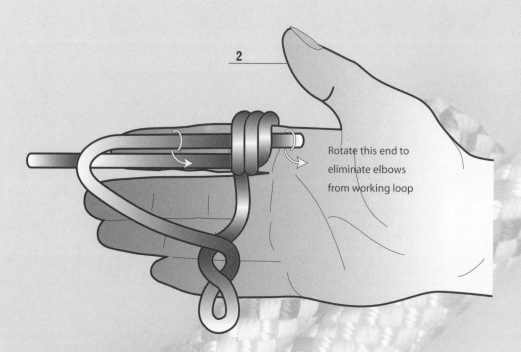

2

Rotate this end to
eliminate elbows
from working loop

METHOD 2

When this binding knot is applied close to the end of
the foundation monofilament, braid, wire or cable, a
different technique can be used which eliminates the
tricky final tuck. If a nail or needle is still used, it is
merely to stiffen the line that is receiving the knot until
it can be completed and tightened. Try it out with cord
on a forefinger. Lay both ends of the line parallel and in

opposite directions as shown (fig. 1) and then take a
couple of wrapping turns with the resulting loop,
passing it over and around the end of whatever
foundation is being seized. Rotate the standing end of
the working loop (in this instance, up at the front and
down at the back) to eliminate the entwined elbows
that have appeared in the working loop (fig. 2); and

<44>

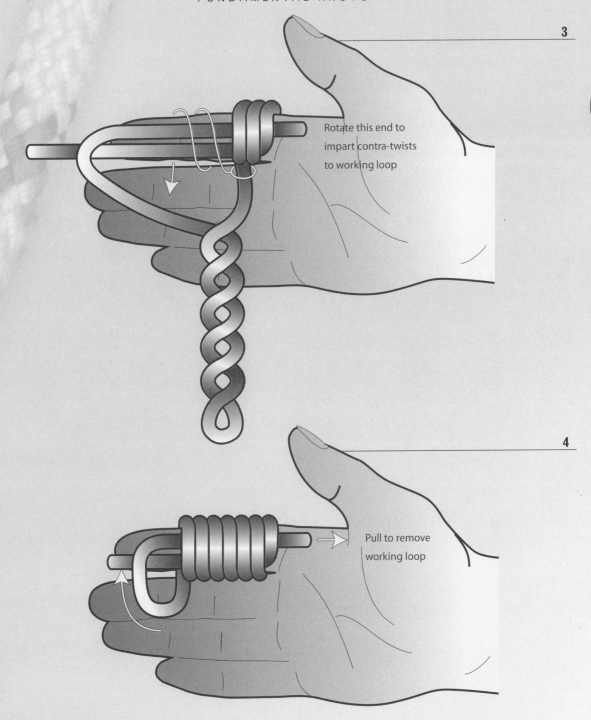

3

Rotate this end to impart contra-twists to working loop

4

Pull to remove working loop

continue rotating it until a number of contra-twists (helixing in the opposite direction to those just eliminated) have been imparted to the loop – one for each intended wrapping turn around the foundation. Continue binding the working loop tightly and snugly

(fig. 3) until the required length of whipping has been achieved, when no twists should be left in the loop. From time to time, when necessary, untangle the free end from the working loop. Pull on the end that will close the loop, then pull on both ends to tighten it (fig. 4).

METHOD 3 (DIRECT)

When a long sequence of wrapping turns are to be tied off (for example, the 20 or more of a Bimini twist), or there is a need to finish off a plaited splice securely, use this whipping variation. Lay the working end back along the knotwork already completed (fig. 1) and continue wrapping with the working loop, as described in method 2. Untangle the free end from the working loop periodically and also remember to rotate the standing end, if necessary, to cope with the torsion that will otherwise result in a twisted loop and that will make it difficult to tighten the knot. Finally, pull on the end to remove the loop and tighten this binding (fig. 2). Cut the tag end flush with the wrapping turns.

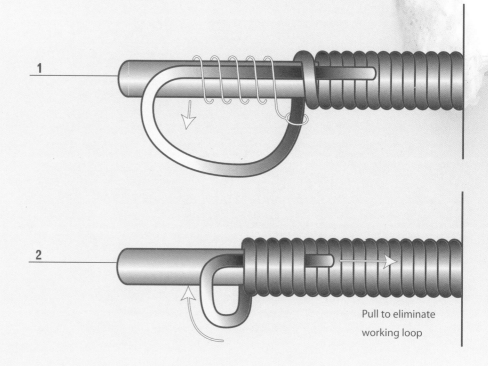

Pull to eliminate working loop

<46>

METHOD 3 (INDIRECT)

For a similar situation, but where the end of the foundation monofilament, braid, wire or cable is not accessible, another approach is possible. Wrap the working end as shown (fig. 1), then pull upon it to invert the wrappings by drawing them inside out. The best word I have heard amongst knot tyers for this technique is 'flyping', which means turning an uncompleted knot inside out (like a sock or glove); this word, which so aptly describes the process, has been in use since the 1890s (and is credited to the mathematician and knot theorist Peter Guthrie Tait). So, the turns are flyped (fig. 2) to resemble half a blood knot, then tightened (fig. 3). This indirect method of tying by flyping is an indispensable technique for tying many fishing knots.

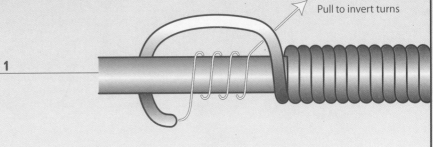

Pull to invert turns

1

Pull

2

3

<47>

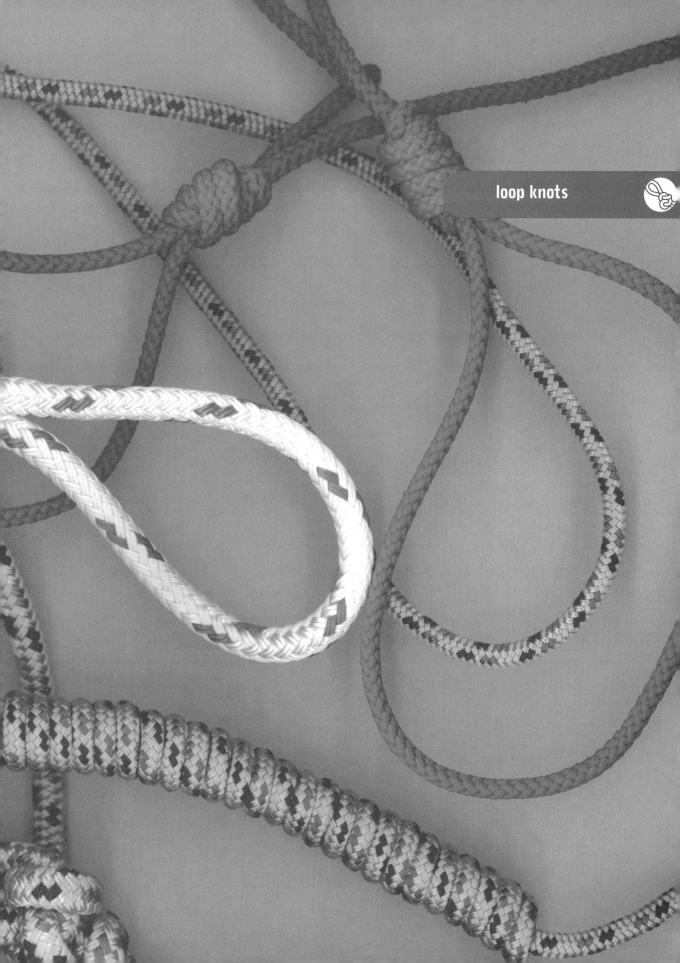

RAPALA KNOT

APPLICATIONS

This knot, like a true lover's knot, makes a small fixed loop that allows a lure to move realistically. It is recommended for plugs, to facilitate their vibrating, darting, erratic actions, but it will suit any sort of lure or fly that needs freedom to wriggle or wobble about enticingly.

METHOD

Tie a simple overhand or thumb knot before passing the working end through the ring or other attachment. Tuck the end back through the initial knot in the opposite direction to how it emerged, creating a skewed slip knot, and adjust the loop to the required size (fig. 1). Wrap and tuck the end repeatedly as shown (figs. 2-4). Work everything tight and snug (fig. 5).

HISTORY

The Rapala company has promoted this knot for use with its products, although they were unable to tell me how or when it originated. The knot was drawn to my attention by Roland Field of Moelfre, Wales on 15th May 1998.

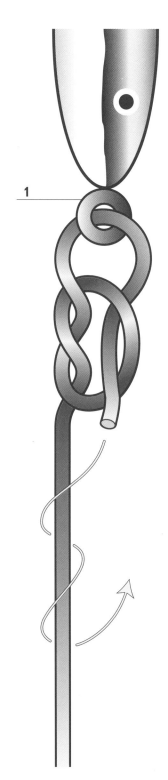

<50>

3

4

5

<51>

ANGLER'S LOOP

APPLICATIONS

This knot may be used to start a tackle system, or hitched directly onto the ring of a hook, lure or swivel. It works in just about any kind of line or leader.

METHOD 1 (DIRECT)

Create the layout illustrated (figs. 1-2) and pull out the uppermost knot part (fig. 3) to make a loop. Adjust this loop to the required size, then tighten the knot. To attach an item of hardware such as a swivel, thread it onto both legs of the loop, pass it through the loop and pull the resulting ring hitch snug against the ring (figs. 4-5).

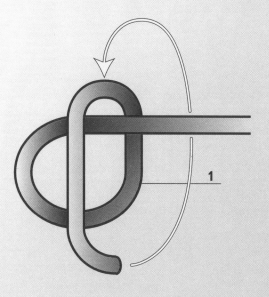

1

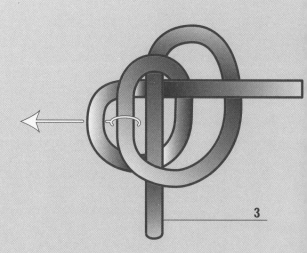

3

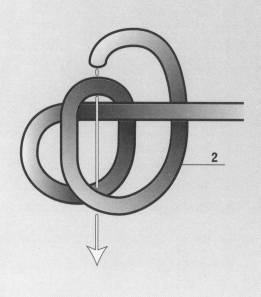

2

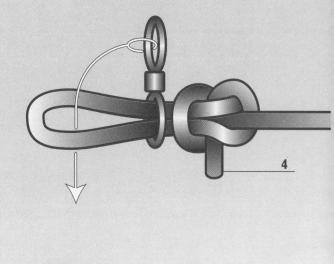

4

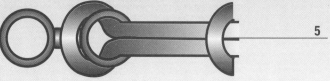

5

<52>

METHOD 2 (INDIRECT)

To attach this loop knot to a ring other than by means of the ring hitch already described, first tie an overhand knot in the line before passing the working end through the ring and back through the overhand knot to make a simple slip knot (fig. 1). Adjust the loop to the required size and tuck the end as shown (fig. 2). Tighten the knot (fig. 3).

HISTORY

This classic angling knot is also referred to as the perfection loop (and by at least one writer as the 'prefect' knot - because it is almost perfect!). It is supposed to date back at least to Izaak Walton in the seventeenth century and certainly worked well in the old-fangled gut, horsehair and silken lines of those days; but it has survived the change to modern materials – indeed, it will even remain secure in elastic bungee (or shock) cord.

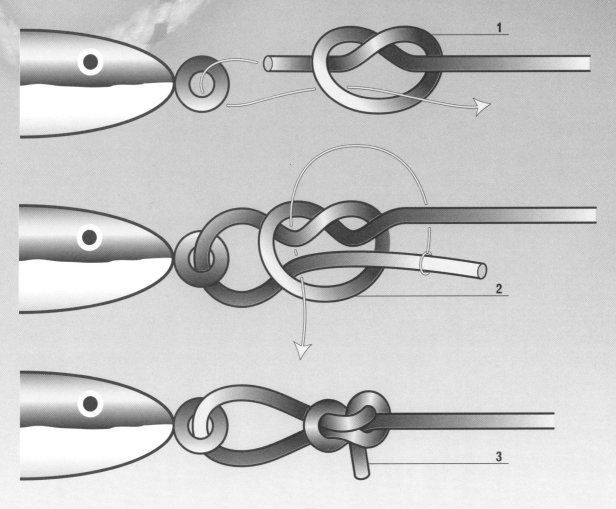

<53>

HANGMAN'S NOOSE

APPLICATIONS

This is a sliding equivalent of the Bimini twist and is another very strong loop knot.

METHOD

The knot may be ring-hitched to any hook, lure or swivel after being tied; but, if only the single line is to be passed through the point of attachment (as illustrated), then it must be done before tying the knot. Next bend the working end back alongside itself to create a long bight (fig. 1).

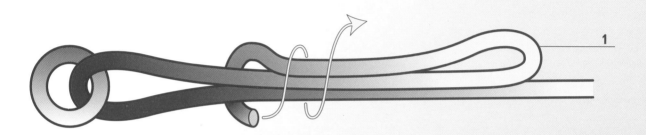

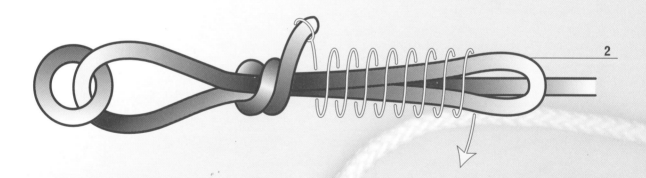

HISTORY

Tied in three-strand hemp rope, this is the gruesome knot brandished by lynch mobs in Hollywood films. It is also known as Jack Ketch's knot after the infamous seventeenth-century hangman immortalised in Punch & Judy shows, although later judicial executioners seem to have preferred something simpler.

<54>

Begin a series of wrapping turns, going away from the hook or other bit of hardware, so as to enclose the standing part of the line and both legs of the bight (fig. 2) which should nest neatly in a triangular cross-section. Complete at least 10 turns, ensuring they lie snugly and neatly together (fig. 3), tuck the end through the bight, and then pull on whichever one of the loop legs closes the bight to trap the tag end. Slide the completed knot along the line to adjust the loop to the required size (fig. 4).

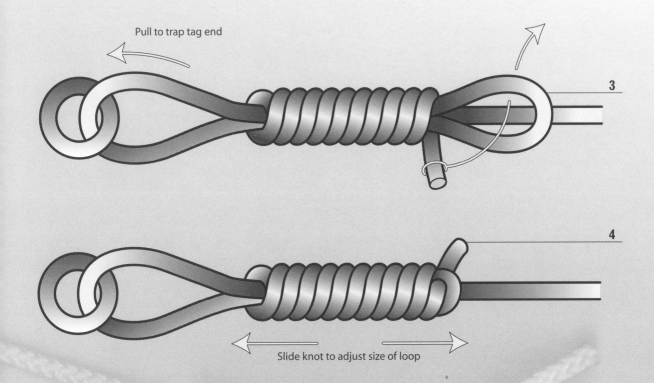

Pull to trap tag end

3

4

Slide knot to adjust size of loop

FIGURE OF EIGHT LOOPS

APPLICATIONS

This trio of loop knots may be used to assemble various rigs in monofilament or braid, either in the basic form (method 1), with an extra half twist (method 2), or with two extra half twists (method 3). They are all quick and easy to tie and the choice is really a matter of which holds best in what materials – the smoother the line, the more twisted the knot.

METHOD 1

Make a long-ish bight in the doubled end of the line and twist it to form a loop (fig. 1). Bring the bight around and tuck it through the loop to complete the distinctive figure of eight layout that gives this knot – and related ones – their names (fig. 2). Pull it tight (fig. 3).

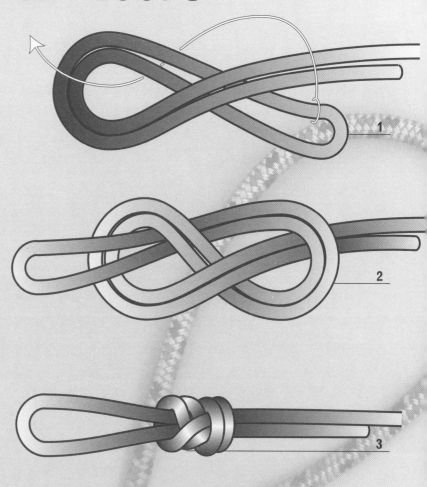

<56>

METHOD 2

Begin as if tying the preceding figure of eight loop (fig. 1), then add another twist to the loop before tucking the bight to complete the knot (figs. 2-3). Tighten (fig. 4).

1

2

3

4

METHOD 3

Double a long length of line and
create a loop by imparting three
half twists to it (fig. 1). Tuck the
bight through the loop (fig. 2) and
then tighten the knot (fig. 3).

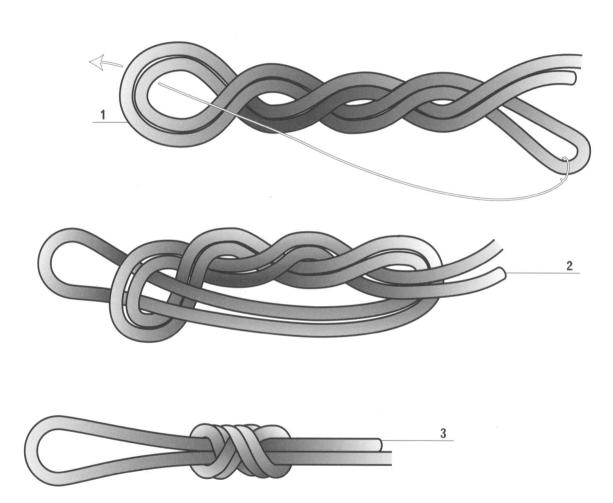

1

2

3

<58>

TRUE LOVER'S KNOT

APPLICATIONS

This knot – briefly introduced in the section on Fundamental Knots – may be quickly and easily tied in monofilament, braid or plastic-coated wire and its small fixed loop allows realistic movement of a plug or other lure. It is a comparatively weak knot, reducing the breaking strength of a line by perhaps 30-50%.

METHOD

Tie an overhand knot, prior to passing the working end of line through the ring forming the point of attachment for this knot. Adjust the loop to its required size and then make a second complementary knot, of identical handedness (but inverted), alongside the first one (figs. 1-2). Tighten both individual knots and slide them together (figs. 3-4).

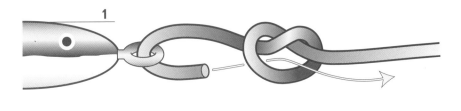

1

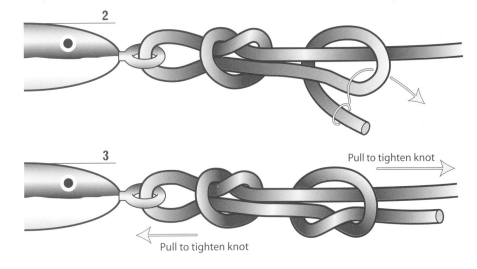

2

3

Pull to tighten knot

Pull to tighten knot

4

HISTORY

In the first century AD this knot was recommended by the Greek physician Herakles as a surgical sling. He knew it as the single *karkhesios*. It re-emerged in medieval literature as a true love (or true lover's) knot and also as the dalliance knot. It has become known to anglers as the Englishman's loop knot or fisherman's loop knot, and – for some unknown reason – in recent decades, as the Homer Rhodes knot.

<59>

DOUBLE OVERHAND LOOP KNOT

APPLICATIONS

This is a fairly strong and secure loop for slick modern materials.

METHOD

Make a long-ish bight in the end of the line and tie the doubled line into a simple overhand knot (fig. 1). Tuck the bight a second time to end up with a double overhand knot (fig. 2). Tighten the knot slowly and carefully, kneading it into the form of a blood knot (fig. 3), at the same time keeping the knot parts parallel to eliminate lumpy distortion of the completed knot. Then finish tightening it (fig. 4).

HISTORY

This knot was never suitable for rope and other large cordage. Its use was limited to string, as a parcel knot for shopkeepers when dry goods all had to be weighed, wrapped and tied for customers. It is a traditional angling knot; one of few to emerge from the days of horsehair and gut and be recommended for nylon monofilament.

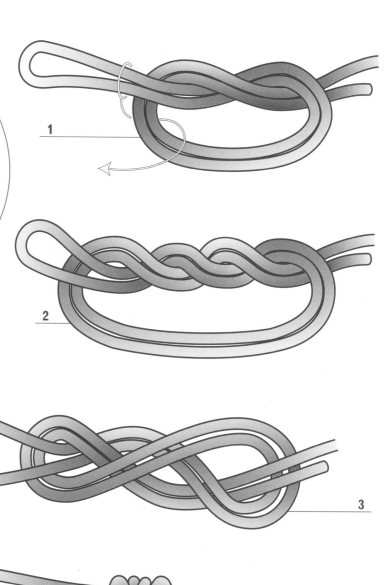

<60>

TRIPLE OVERHAND LOOP KNOT

APPLICATIONS

This is a chunkier and stronger version of the preceding knot. Even more turns may be added, when it will do instead of a Bimini twist (see p. 66). The extra tuck(s) would not have been required in the days of gut and horsehair. Indeed the double overhand loop knot was still being recommended in the early 1950s by manufacturers of the new-fangled synthetic fishing lines. But lines are now even slicker and so increased friction is demanded from the knots used in them. A multiple overhand loop is widely known as the surgeon's loop, but the angling application is also called the thumb loop, spider knot or loop and sometimes (quite wrongly) spider hitch.

METHOD

Make a long bight in the end of the line and tie a double overhand knot (fig. 1). Add a third tuck to make a triple overhand knot (fig. 2) and begin the tightening process that will convert it into a blood knot, taking care to remove unwanted twists in the doubled lines. Finally tighten the knot (fig. 3). It is claimed by some that this knot is easier to tie than a Bimini twist – and it certainly requires less by way of hands and feet – but it can easily be botched and emerge as a bird's nest of tangled coils.

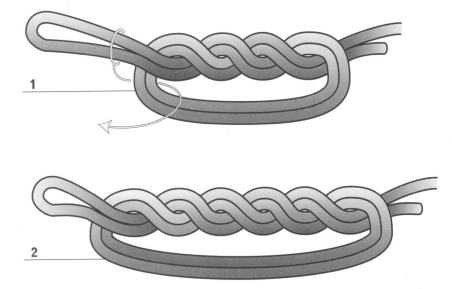

1

2

3

<61>

TROMBONE LOOP

APPLICATIONS

In conditions when the preceding multiple overhand (or surgeon's) loop proves troublesome to tie, fall back upon this easier alternative. If breaking strength is a critical consideration, however, be aware that the abrupt angle of the final tuck weakens this knot.

METHOD

Create a long bight in the doubled end of the line and make a large loop with it (fig. 1). Begin to wrap the bight around the loop (fig. 2), ensuring that the doubled lines remain parallel and lie neatly and snugly beside one another. Tuck the single bight through the doubled loop (fig. 3) and trap it there by pulling the standing part and tag end together to close the loop tight (fig. 4).

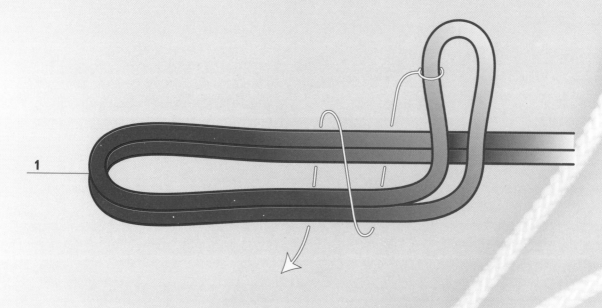

1

HISTORY

The name refers to the long but retractable (trombone-like) bight, doubled in this instance, with which the knot is tied; and there is an entire family (of which the hangman's noose is another member) of related knots which it might be helpful to label collectively 'trombone knots', thus adding a useful sub-group to existing knot classification.

 <62>

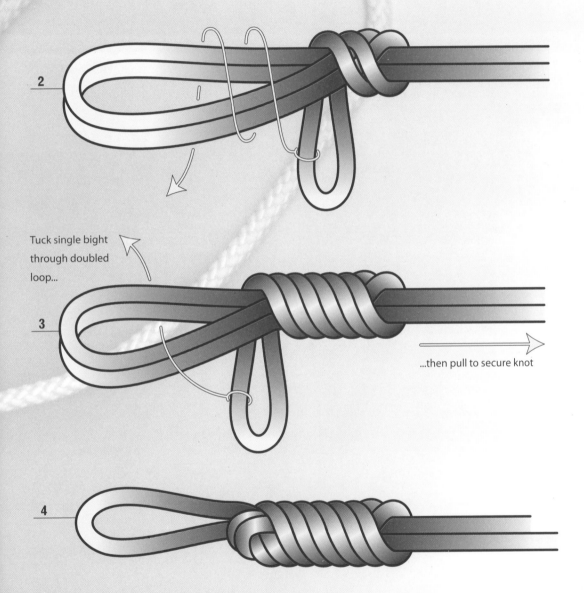

2

Tuck single bight
through doubled
loop...

3

...then pull to secure knot

4

<63>

PLAITED OR BRAIDED LOOP

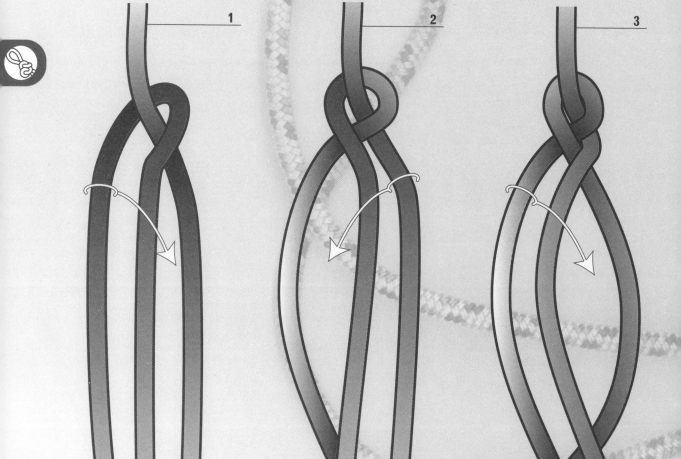

1

2

3

Untangle tag end
as necessary

APPLICATIONS

This is claimed to be one of the strongest of all loops
(100% – that is, as strong as the unknotted line) and it
is recommended for the start of any tackle system
intended for deep-sea, blue-water big game fishing.

METHOD

Lay out the line as shown (fig. 1) and bring the left-
hand part of it over (in front) to become the new centre
strand. Next bring the right-hand strand over to

<64>

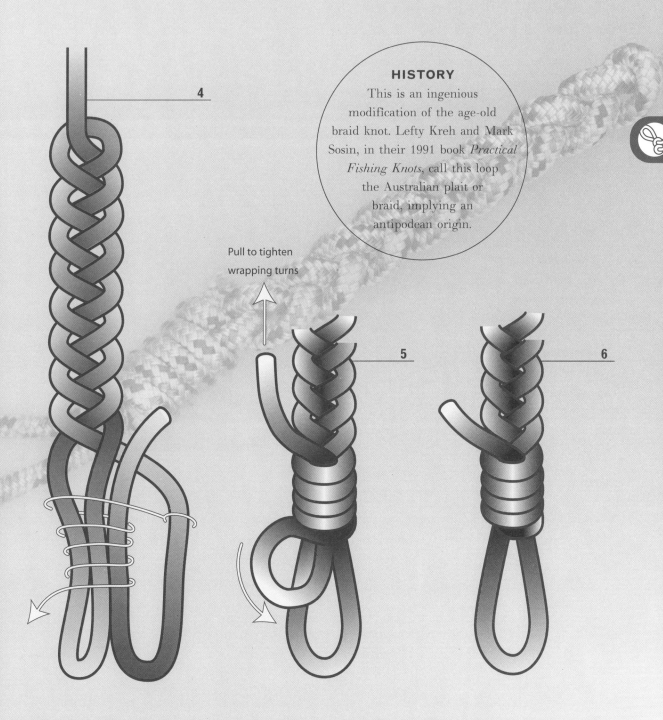

4

Pull to tighten
wrapping turns

5

6

become the centre strand (fig. 2). Then bring the left-hand strand over to become the centre strand (fig. 3). Repeat stages 2 and 3 to create a three-strand pigtail plait or braid. Note how a loosely interwoven mirror image of this plait becomes tangled lower down in the long bight – and pull out the standing end periodically to eliminate this unwanted complication. When several

centimetres (or inches) of plait have been made, turn what has so far been the working end back on itself and then take at least four or five wrapping turns with the same strand around both loop legs and its own end (fig. 4). Close up the smaller loop thus created by pulling on the tag end (fig. 5) and so fully tightening the whipping to complete this loop knot (fig. 6).

<65>

BIMINI TWIST

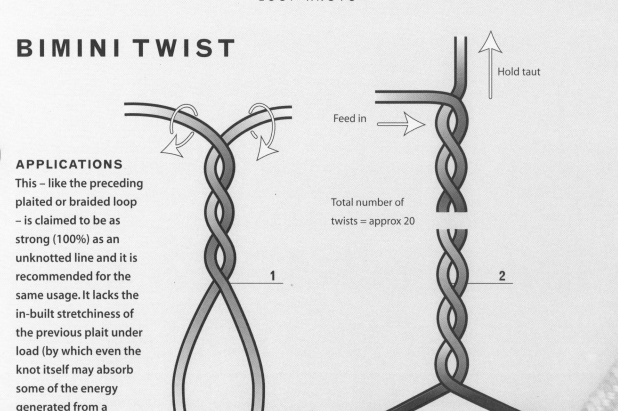

APPLICATIONS

This – like the preceding plaited or braided loop – is claimed to be as strong (100%) as an unknotted line and it is recommended for the same usage. It lacks the in-built stretchiness of the previous plait under load (by which even the knot itself may absorb some of the energy generated from a sudden strike by a fish).

METHOD

Double the line into a bight that is at least 1m (3ft) long and twist 20 or so turns into it (fig. 1). The loop must now be pulled forcibly outwards to compress the initial twists (fig. 2); and, since both hands will be needed elsewhere, this entails using the feet or knees (or a partner). Hold the standing part of the line firmly in one hand, while the fingers of the other hand pull the working end out at right-angles to it, and as the loop is forced open counter-turns will be created at the upper end of the twists (fig. 3).

Feed the accumulating secondary layer of wrapping turns neatly downwards towards the loop. Finish off the knot in one of two ways. Either add a couple of half hitches (fig. 4) or apply at least five or six seizing turns over a doubled back tag end (fig. 5) which must then be pulled tight (fig. 6).

<66>

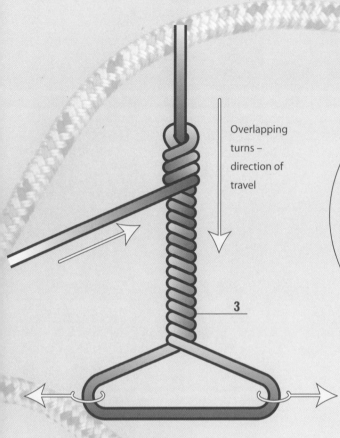

Overlapping turns – direction of travel

3

HISTORY
The Bimini twist is a comparative newcomer to knotting literature, having first been described by Lefty Krey and Mark Sosin in their 1975 book *Practical Fishing & Boating Knots*. The name is presumably an exotic reference to Bimini Island in the Bahamas, where blue-water big game fishing demands the most robust of knots.

4

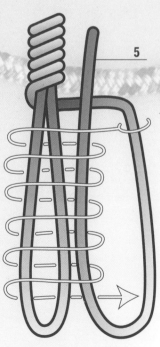

5

Pull to remove slack and secure knot

6

<67>

ONE-WAY SHEET BEND

APPLICATIONS

This knot secures the end of one line to a pre-tied loop knot in another, in such a way that the tag end does not project at right-angles to disturb the water but is streamlined. It may be used in lines of somewhat dissimilar size, in which case the thicker of the two should form the loop. For lines that differ greatly in thickness or stiffness, other knots will be described later in this section.

HISTORY

Remnants of Stone Age nets contain mesh knots resembling sheet bends, so Neolithic man may have known this knot. It has appeared in seamanship manuals since 1794. Clifford Ashley was shown this streamlined angling application by Richard S. Whitney, as the Lorn knot. In *Fisherman's Knots & Wrinkles* (1927), W.A. Hunter illustrated it unnamed (and, inexplicably, with the loop in the thinner of the two lines). It is sometimes called a tucked sheet bend.

METHOD

Insert the working end of one line through the other loop. Pass it around behind both loop legs and back across in front to tuck beneath itself (figs. 1-2), making a basic sheet bend. Then tuck the end a second time, into a figure of eight layout and tighten the knot (fig. 3).

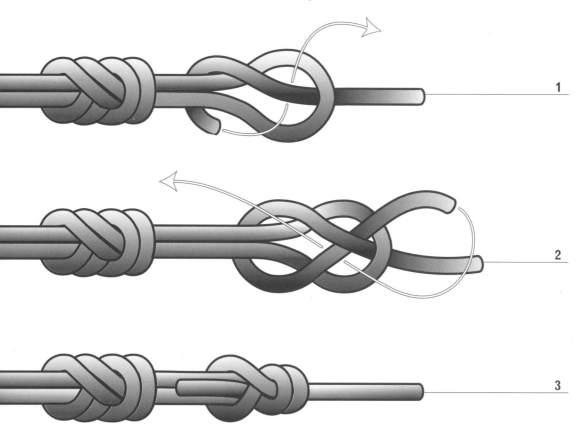

1

2

3

<70>

ALBRIGHT KNOT

APPLICATIONS

Use this knot to join lines of different diameters or materials. For example, join a fly line to a leader, monofilament to braid, or braid to wire.

METHOD

Make a bight in the thicker of the two lines. Insert and wrap the thinner one around towards the end of the bight (figs. 1-2), taking care that each overlying wrapping turn lies snugly and neatly beside the preceding one, while the three inert parts they contain nest neatly in triangular cross-section. Ten or twelve turns may be needed in a single line (more than are illustrated) but six or seven may be enough in a thin doubled line. Lastly, tuck the working end through the bight (fig. 3) and draw everything tight (fig. 4). Some anglers recommend tying the tag end of the lighter line to its own standing part; while even stricter adherents of the belt-&-braces approach suggest, when using super-braid for the loop, that its tag end should also be secured to its own standing part.

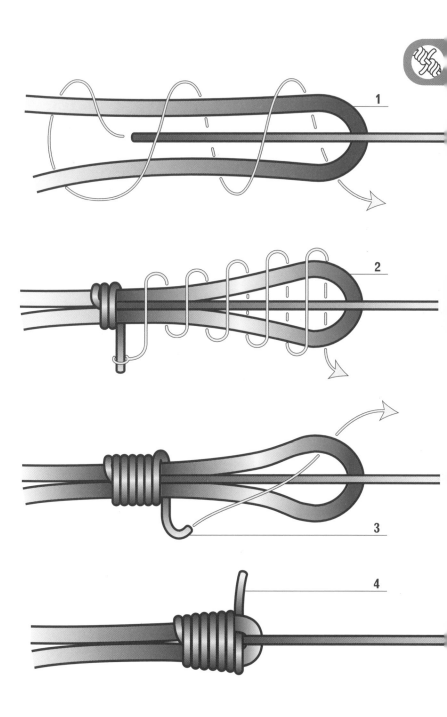

1

2

3

4

HISTORY

This knot (also called the Albright special) has been around the angling scene for over 20 years. It is credited to Jimmy Albright, a guide in the Florida Keys.

<71>

SEIZING BEND

APPLICATIONS

This little-known newcomer to the knotting repertoire is well worth a try for joining lines of greatly dissimilar diameters.

HISTORY

This knot has been recommended for boating and wilderness pioneering, as well as less demanding outdoor activities, but not – until now – for angling. It was intended to be a robust heaving line knot, for when a lightweight throwing line must be used as a 'messenger' to haul a much heavier working rope into position up a height, across an intervening space, or over some other intervening obstacle. The inventive Harry Asher's[IGKT] fertile mind and fingers devized the seizing bend and first described it in *A New System of Knotting*, published in 1986 by the International Guild of Knot Tyers.

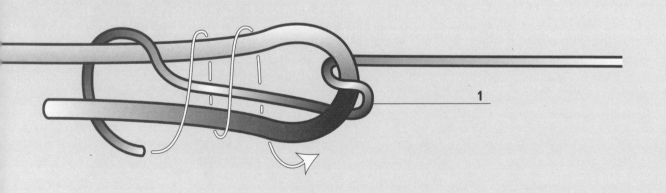

1

<72>

METHOD

Make a bight in the bigger of the two lines and take a
turn around it with the lesser line. Apply wrapping
turns, keeping them neat and snugly together, which
progress towards the end of the bight (figs. 1-2). Next
extend the initial turn in the thinner line and loop it
over the short end of the bight in the larger line (fig. 3)
to create a tensioning turn that holds everything else
in place. Then tighten the knot (fig. 4). As with the
preceding Albright knot, some individuals may deem it
prudent to tie one or both ends to their own standing
parts (not illustrated).

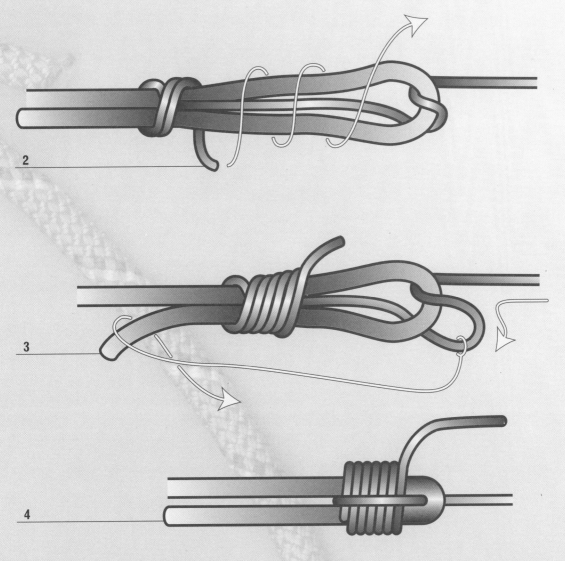

<73>

INTERLOCKED LOOPS

APPLICATIONS

Linked loops are secure because there are no ends to
come free and the interlocked parts remove much of
the strain from the actual knots that make those
loops. They can be used to join very different sorts
of lines.

<74>

Lark's head layout

4

METHOD 1 (DIRECT)

Use this quick and easy method (figs. 1-3), which requires little or no explanation, when the standing end of one of the two lines is easily accessible, because it is not too long or it is neatly coiled or spooled. Do not allow the knot to capsize into a lark's head layout (fig. 4), which concentrates the load into a smaller area and so may weaken it.

<75>

INTERLOCKED LOOPS

METHOD 2 (INDIRECT)

When neither standing end is available, it will be necessary to tie the end of one line into the other loop. First make an overhand knot about 15cm (6in) from the working end, then weave and tuck the end as shown (figs. 1-2). Complete a classic angler's loop and ensure that any load will fall equally upon all four legs of both loops (fig. 3). Once again, avoid a weak lark's head layout (see method 1 – fig. 4) .

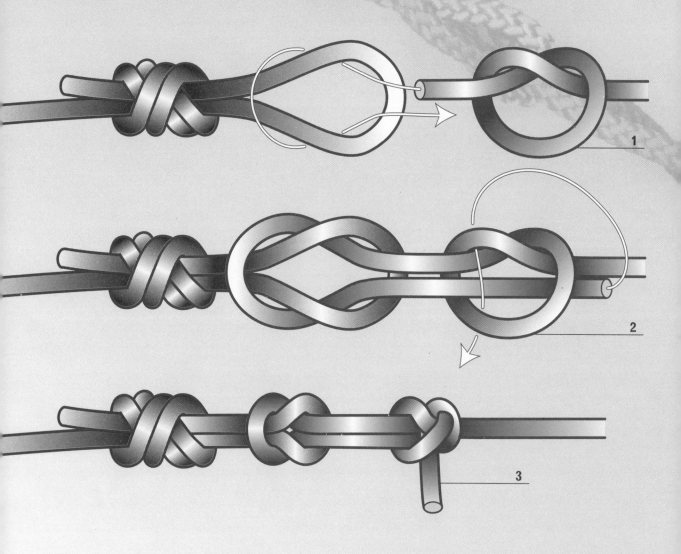

<76>

METHOD 3 (INDIRECT)

The flat knot that results from the preceding descriptions (methods 1 & 2) does not flex and bend with equal ease in all directions, whereas this alternative behaves more like a couple of chain links or a universal coupling. As it never jams tight, this layout may even be fractionally stronger. Interweave the working end of one line through the loop of the other exactly as illustrated (figs. 1-3) – having first tied an overhand knot (see method 2) about 15cm (6in) from that end – then tie off the tag end on its own standing part by completing the angler's loop.

HISTORY

Most children discover how (by method 1) to make elastic band chains with a series of these flat knots, so it seems likely that humankind could have discovered interlocked loops at a very early date. Although the knot looks like a reef (square) knot, its dynamics are different, due to a load being spread evenly over all four legs of both loops. Method 3 incorporates a carrick bend configuration, a knot that can be traced back to Ireland in the Elizabethan era.

1

2

Knot tag end to standing part of line

3

HUFFNAGLE KNOT

APPLICATIONS

This burly combination of a fisherman's knot and a half-blood knot is used to join a light fly leader tippet to a very heavy 36-54kg (80-120lb) monofilament. The knot has emerged in recent years from the Florida Keys, widely publicized and recommended for joining heavy lines to lighter ones. My instinctive reaction is that a fisherman's knot is the wrong one for dissimilar lines; and the fact that users feel the need to beef it up with a half blood knot reinforces not just the knot but also my antipathy for it. It seems a clumsy contrivance. I am advised, however, that those guides and clients who go leagues offshore into deep blue seas for big game are impressed by its performance, so I will limit further comment to a suggestion that the knot on the next page, the plaited interlocked loop, might prove a more elegant alternative.

METHOD

Tie the end of the heavy line to a long loop of the lighter one with a fisherman's knot, using both legs of the loop to make one of the two overhand knots (fig. 1). Take two-and-a-half wraps with the working loop around the standing part of the larger line (fig. 2), then turn them inside out (i.e. flype them, like peeling off a sock or glove) to form a half blood knot. Tighten this compound knot and trim to end up with four tag ends (fig. 3).

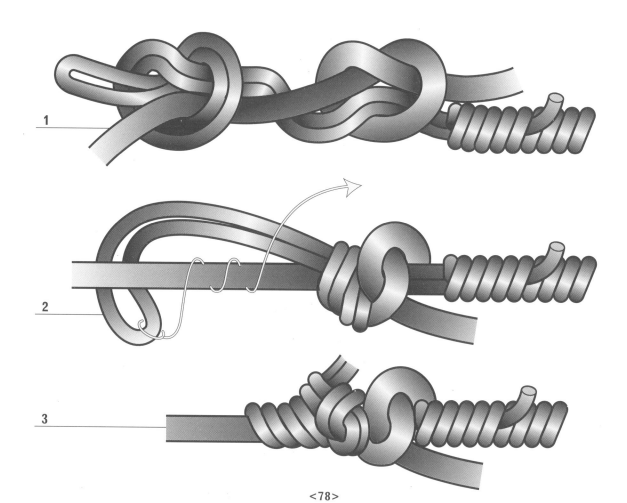

1

2

3

<78>

PLAITED INTERLOCKED LOOPS

APPLICATIONS

A strong yet streamlined joining knot, included here as an alternative to the huffnagle knot. This layout may be tied in lines of the same size and type, but it will also cope well with lines of very different diameters and materials. It never fully tightens but remains flexible.

HISTORY

This knot uses two lines to replicate the four-strand square plait once used for the flex attached to vintage telephones. It is not commonly used in angling.

METHOD

Twist at least four loops into a bight of one line, tying it with a fixed loop knot, and then tie a figure of eight knot about 30cm (1ft) away from the end of the other line (fig. 1). Insert the working end up through the first loop, down through the second, up through the third and down through the fourth, in the manoeuvre known in knot tying parlance as ply-splitting. Continue for as long as there are loops through which the working end can porpoise up and down. Before starting the working end on its return journey, identify the direction of twist in the initial loops – in this instance right-handed or clockwise. The working end must go in the opposite direction – that is, left-handed or anti(counter)-clockwise. Tuck exactly as shown (fig. 2) to produce an interwoven counter-twist. This plait will only retain its form and function when the load is applied evenly on both legs at each end, so the working end must be inserted through the original figure of eight knot to follow the original lead of this knot until it has been doubled (fig. 3). Pull the interwoven loops tight without necessarily having them close up against the loop knots. If both loops were to twist in the same direction, the result would be a twined-&-twisted ligature knot (see p. 88).

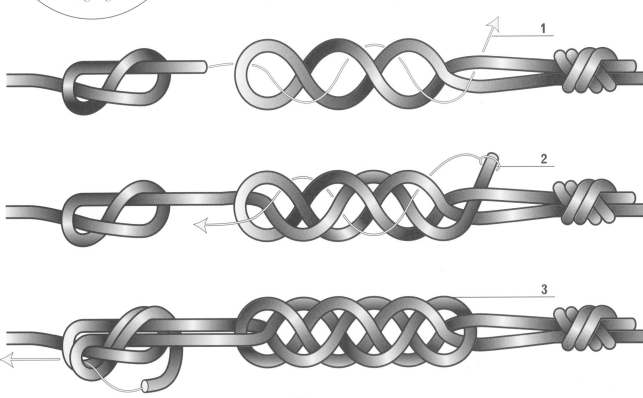

<79>

WATER KNOT

APPLICATIONS
Attach a leader to a reel line, or
any line to another, with this knot.

METHOD 1 (DIRECT)
Bring both tag ends together and
tie a basic half knot (fig. 1), in this
instance left-handed. Tuck each
end in turn (fig. 2) to complete the
knot, keeping both lines parallel
throughout. Arrange it so that the
tag ends emerge (in this
illustration) at the bottom of the
knot – since there is evidence it is
stronger this way – then tighten
the knot (fig. 3).

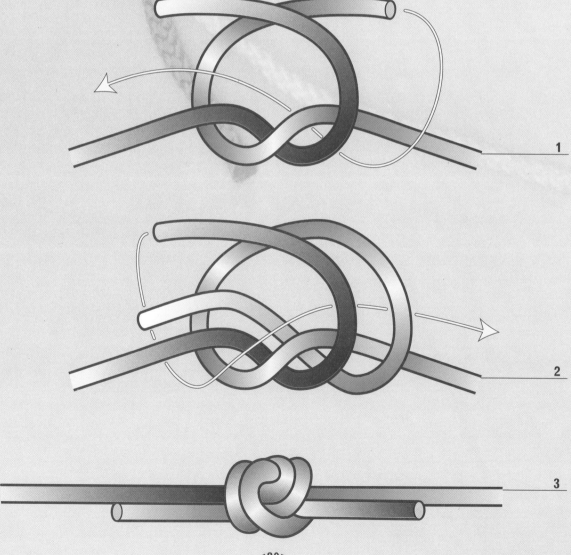

1

2

3

<80>

METHOD 2 (INDIRECT)

Tie an overhand knot in the end of one of the lines to be joined, then insert the working end of the other line through this knot and follow it around until it has been duplicated (figs. 1-2). Both tag ends should be made to emerge at the top of the knot in this example, as the knot may be stronger when tied this way. Take care that the two lines remain parallel throughout, removing any unwanted twists, and then tighten the knot (fig. 3).

HISTORY

The earliest reference to this knot was in *Treatyse of Fyshinge wyth an Angle*, reputedly by Dame Juliana Berners (or Barnes), Prioress of Sopwell, and printed in 1496. It is a trusted angling knot from the days of horsehair and gut. Some writers believe Izaak Walton favoured this knot, but his seminal seventeenth-century book *The Compleat Angler* does not portray or refer to one knot. Climbers and cavers use it; it is the only knot recommended for joining the flat tape or webbing used in climbing harnesses.

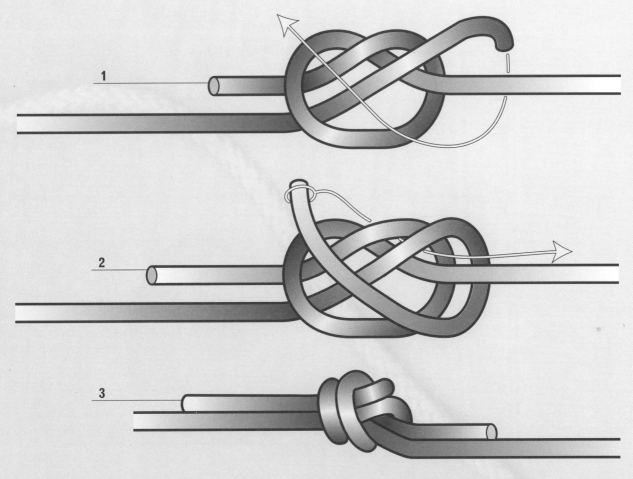

<81>

METHOD 3 (TRIPLE TUCKED)

This triple-tucked variation of the basic knot is bulkier and spreads the load over a larger area. It may be somewhat stronger and is certainly more secure. The method is more handily tied when the end of the longer line can be pulled repeatedly through the belly of the knot. Place the two lines parallel to one another and make an anticlockwise overhand loop in both of them. Tuck both lines once through the loop to make an overhand knot (fig. 1), then twice more for a triple tucked overhand knot. Begin to tighten the knot, kneading it into the characteristic form of a blood knot (fig. 2) and gradually removing all of the slack to tighten fully (fig. 3). If one or both of the long ends make the foregoing direct process impractical, then it may be tied indirectly (method 2) by tying a triple overhand knot in the end of one strand only, introducing the other end and following the lead of the original knot until it has been doubled.

<82>

DOUBLE FISHERMAN'S KNOT

APPLICATIONS

This reinforced version of the basic knot is for lines of the same size and similar materials.

Sometime around 1980, I was conducting a knot-tying workshop for young people in the National Maritime Museum at Greenwich, London, when a boy asked me if I knew "...the knot for cutting fishes''eads orf wiv?" He showed me this one, miming the insertion of a fish between the two knots, then vigorously tugging the knot shut with the grisly glee of a piscine executioner.

METHOD

Lay the two lines parallel and together, overlapping the ends to be tied. Make a double overhand knot in one end around the standing part of the other line and tighten it (figs. 1-2). Turn the work end-for-end and repeat the process with the other end (fig. 3) so that both knots are of identical handedness. Then slide them together (fig. 4).

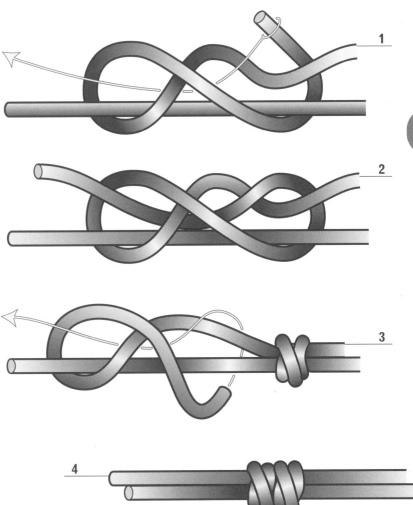

HISTORY

An established fishing knot, this knot has also earned the approval of climbers and cavers. It is referred to by anglers as the grinner knot, presumably from the gaping mouth that appears between the two individual knots prior to sliding them closed, and it is yet another knot to have survived from the gut and horsehair days of fishing.

<83>

TRIPLE FISHERMAN'S KNOT

APPLICATIONS

For joining lines of equal diameter and similar materials, climbers and anglers alike judge this variant to be stronger than the double fisherman's knot. Despite being noticeably bulkier than the doubled version, it will pass through rod guides of the same diameter. The knot is also known as a double grinner knot. In the past it was hardly ever used in natural fibre rope, because it jammed and could not be untied, but this very quality may commend it to anglers.

METHOD

Having mastered the double fisherman's knot just described, this heftier variation of it simply replaces the double overhand knots with a couple of triple-tucked knots (figs. 1-3).

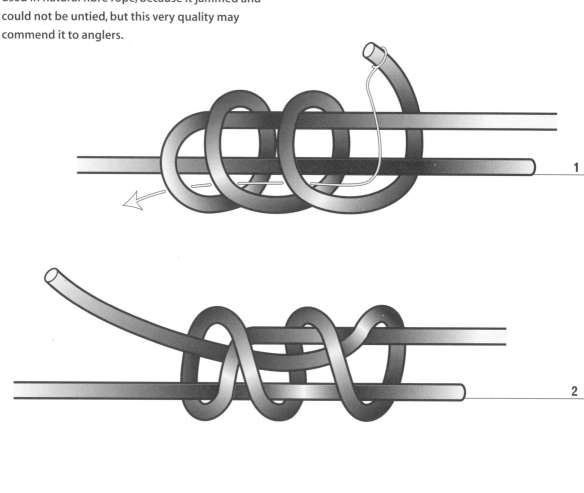

1

2

3

<84>

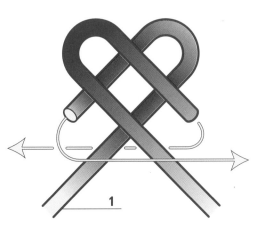

LINFIT KNOT

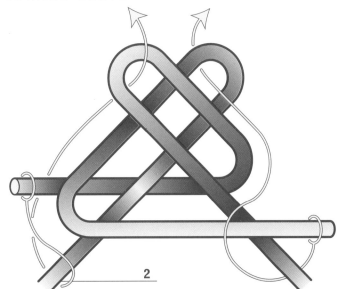

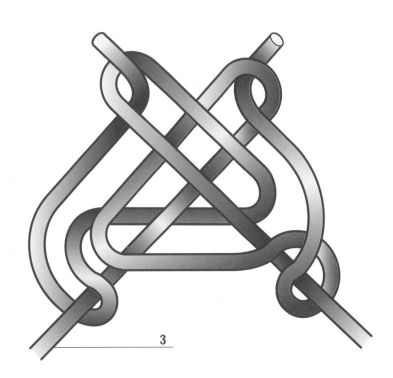

APPLICATIONS

This is a relatively recent alternative to the fisherman's (grinner) knot. It is best suited to thick, hard and springy line, for which it was devised.

METHOD

Make matching bights in both lines and superimpose them as shown (fig. 1). Wrap and tuck both working ends (figs. 2-3), leaving long working ends to absorb the considerable amount of slippage that occurs during the tightening process. Allow the knot to snug down into its finished form (fig. 4), and tighten.

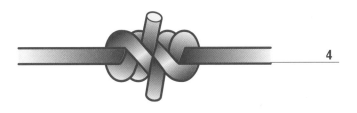

HISTORY

Angler Owen K. Nuttall[IGKT] of Linthwaite, Huddersfield, in West Yorkshire, England discovered this knot, which he described in *Knotting Matters*, the quarterly journal of the International Guild of Knot Tyers, in April 1993.

<85>

BLOOD KNOT

APPLICATIONS

This is a fairly strong knot when it joins lines of the same diameter. In lines of unequal size, the thinner of the two should be used double, when the knot's strength increases slightly.

METHOD 1 (DIRECT – INWARD COILS)

Overlap the ends of the two lines and wrap one working end three or more times back around both its own standing part and the other line. Tuck and trap the tag end between both lines (fig. 1). Repeat the process with the other end and make sure that the second tag end is tucked in the opposite direction to the first one between both lines (fig. 2). Carefully draw this compound and symmetrical knot snug and tight (fig. 3).

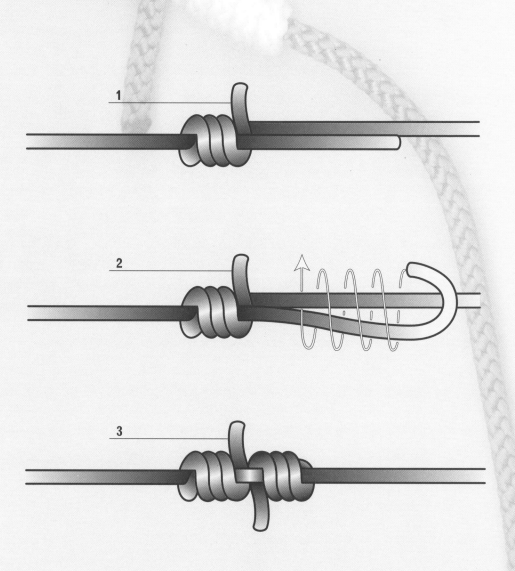

<86>

METHOD 2 (INDIRECT – OUTWARD COILS)

Some angling knot devotees claim this method is preferable. Overlap the two working ends and twist at least three turns with one of them (fig. 1). Bring the tag end around and tuck it back up between the two lines prior to the initial twist (fig. 2). Repeat the process with the other end, taking care to tuck it the opposite way to the first one (fig. 2). Pull the knot tight (fig. 3), so that the wrapping turns unwind and capsize, transforming themselves into a typical couple of half blood knots.

HISTORY

W.A. Hunter reported this knot was shown to him by W.D. Coggeshall on Coggeshall's return from a visit to the USA. In *Angler's Knots* in Gut and Nylon (1948), however, Stanley Barnes claims the construction method was painstakingly worked out by Jock Purvis, a ship engineer, using a microscope to analyse cut sections of knots cast in paraffin wax. Purvis's findings were published by A.H. Chaytor in his *Letters to a Salmon Fisher's Son* (1910).

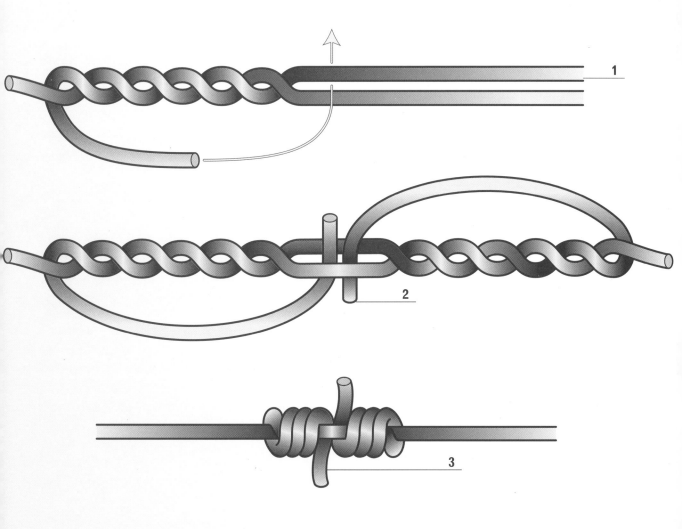

<87>

LIGATURE KNOT (TWINED-&-TWISTED)

APPLICATIONS

Use this knot to join two lines of identical size and type. The number of tucks or turns given to this knot will vary with the sort of line in which it is tied – there will be fewer in thicker, stiffer stuff. The illustrations are, therefore, only one instance of how the knot might appear.

METHOD

Cross both working ends and tuck each one around the adjacent standing part of its partner (fig. 1). Tuck both working ends similarly a second time – and as many times after that as required (the optimum number for maximum strength is said by some to be seven) – in this example twining left-handed or anti(counter)-clockwise (fig. 2).

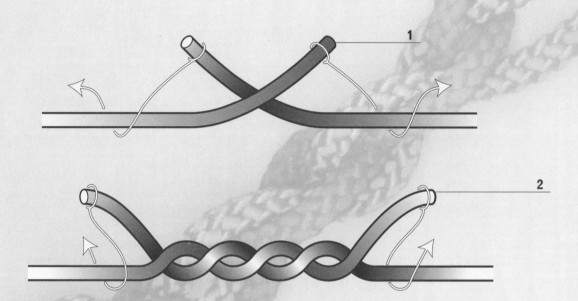

Then cross the working ends again in exactly the same way (in the illustrations, left over right) and take one tuck with each (fig. 3). Continue to tuck (fig. 4) until the upper row of twists matches those in the lower row (fig. 5), both in number and direction, and begin to tighten the knot by pulling a bit at a time on each one of the two working ends and two standing parts in turn. At this stage the knot will start to twist (fig. 6). Allow it to do so; indeed, continue tightening until the knot is twined and twisted as compactly as possible (fig. 7). This knot works best with each tag end secured to its own adjacent standing part, when it becomes effectively an elaborate loop-to-loop arrangement. If each layer of this knot was mistakenly tied with an opposite handedness, the result would be the basis for the plaited interlocked loops described earlier in this section.

HISTORY

Lefty Kreh and Mark Sosin featured this knot in their 1991 book *Practical Fishing Knots*, but refer to it merely as a modification of the simple blood knot. It is in fact a multiple form of another knot altogether – the ligature knot – as the name assigned to it here makes clear.

<88>

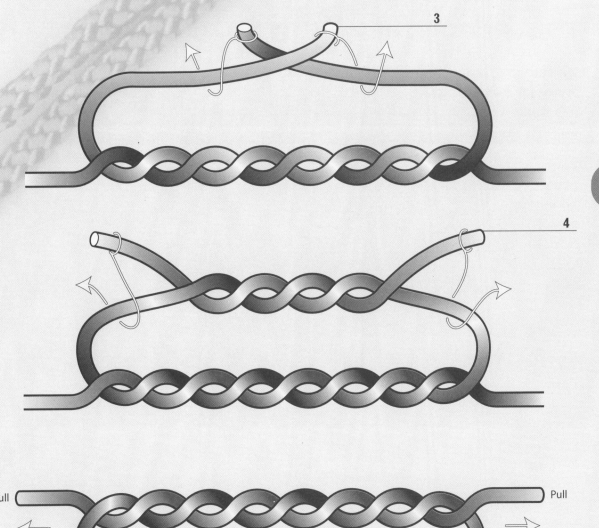

3

4

Pull

Pull

5

Pull

Pull

6

7

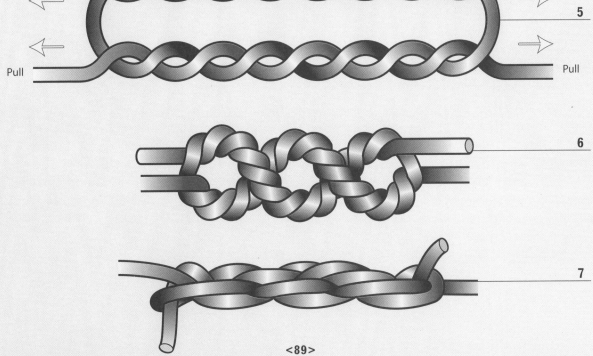

<89>

PLAITED OR BRAIDED SPLICE

APPLICATIONS

Joining two lines in this way ensures great strength and so will occasionally repay the extra time it takes to tie. (See also Plaited or braided loop on page 64.)

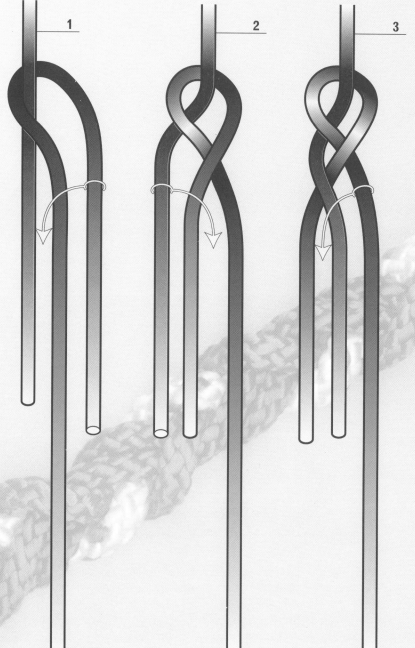

METHOD

Bring together both working ends of the lines to be joined and arrange them as shown (fig. 1), preparatory to making a three-strand plait. Both working ends should be about the same length. Bring the right-hand outer one of the three resulting strands over (across in front of) its own standing part to become the centre strand. Then bring the left-hand outer strand over its neighbour to become the centre strand (fig. 2). Now bring the right-hand outer strand over the adjacent strand to become – in its turn – the new centre strand (fig. 3); and then

<90>

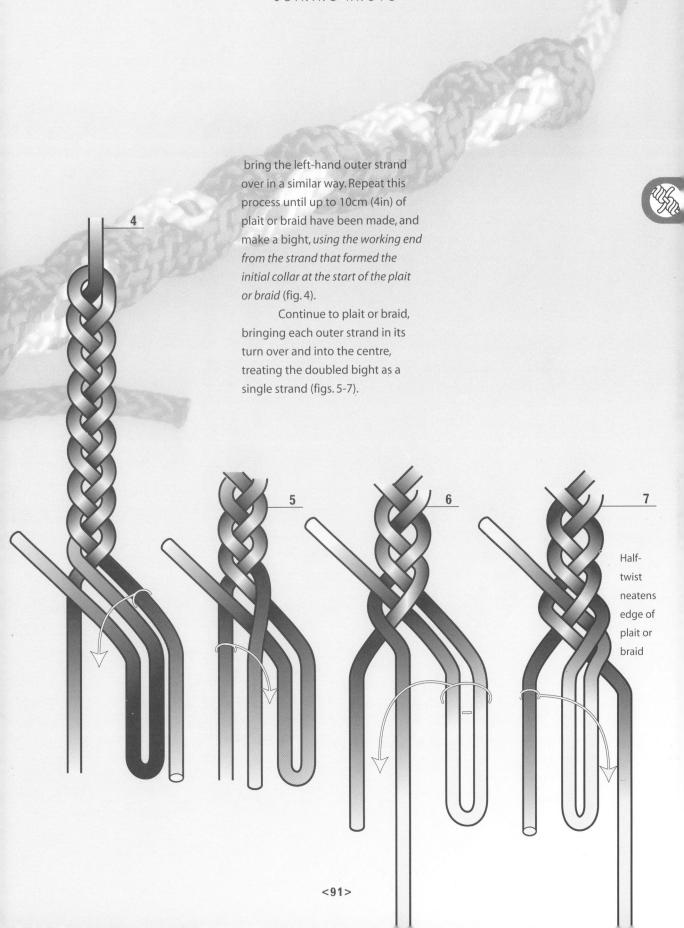

bring the left-hand outer strand over in a similar way. Repeat this process until up to 10cm (4in) of plait or braid have been made, and make a bight, *using the working end from the strand that formed the initial collar at the start of the plait or braid* (fig. 4).

Continue to plait or braid, bringing each outer strand in its turn over and into the centre, treating the doubled bight as a single strand (figs. 5-7).

4

5

6

7

Half-twist neatens edge of plait or braid

<91>

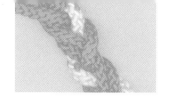

HISTORY

This neat contrivance appeared in Geoff Wilson's *Complete Book of Fishing Knots & Rigs*, published in 1995 by Australian Fishing Network, and for that reason is referred to as the Australian plaited or braided splice.

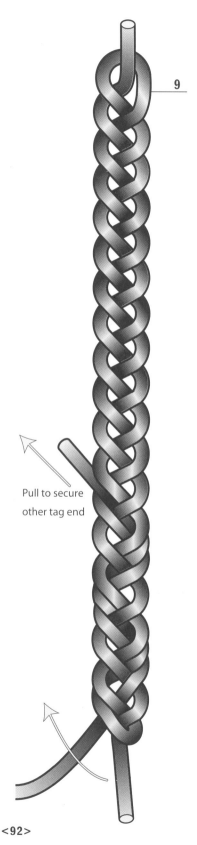

9

When the bight is almost exhausted, tuck the remaining working end down through it (fig. 8) and then trap it securely by pulling carefully on the opposite tag end (fig. 9).

Pull to secure other tag end

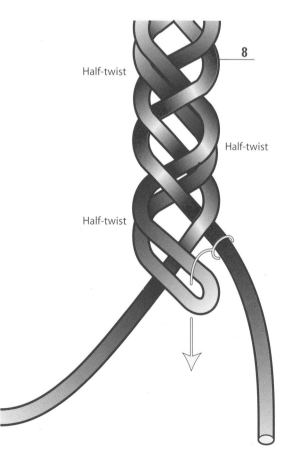

8

Half-twist

Half-twist

Half-twist

<92>

VICE VERSA

APPLICATIONS

Even intractable materials, such as elastic (bungee) shock cords and slimy wet leather thongs, can be held captive with this knot. It has never (as far as I know) been recommended as an angling knot; but, with each tag end lying streamlined alongside its own standing part, it could prove quite suitable in the miniaturized world of fishing lines.

METHOD

Overlap the working ends of the two lines to be joined, wrapping and tucking their working ends as shown (fig. 1). Ensure the completed interwoven layout is as illustrated and then tighten the knot (fig. 2).

1

2

HISTORY

This is another knot from the prolific knot-tying of retired research scientist, the late Harry Asher[IGKT], who discovered it while working systematically through derivations from the common sheet bend and published it in *The Alternative Knot Book* (1989).

<93>

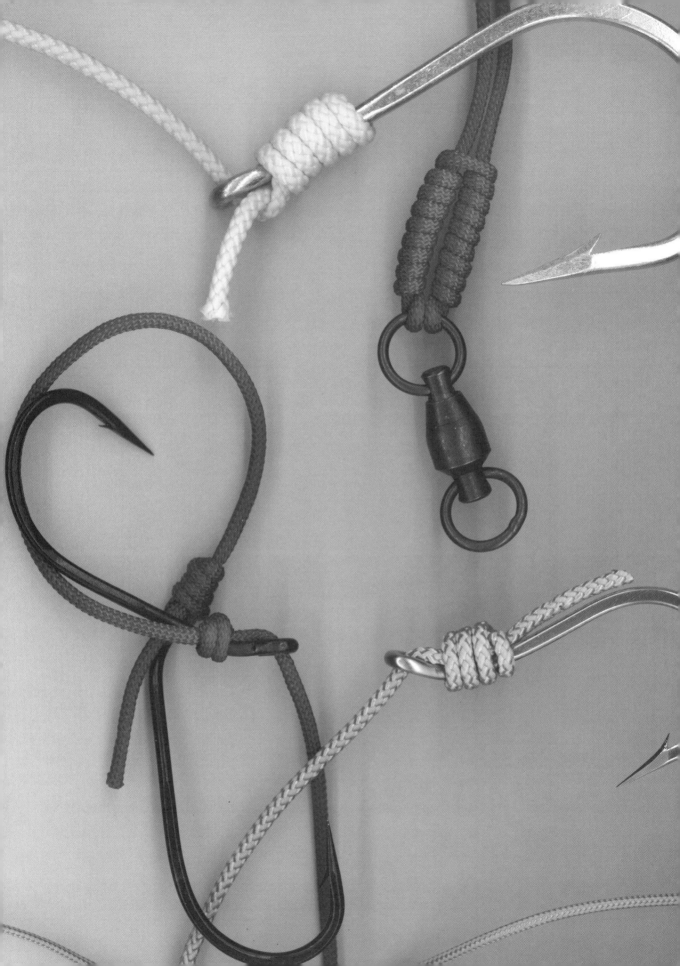

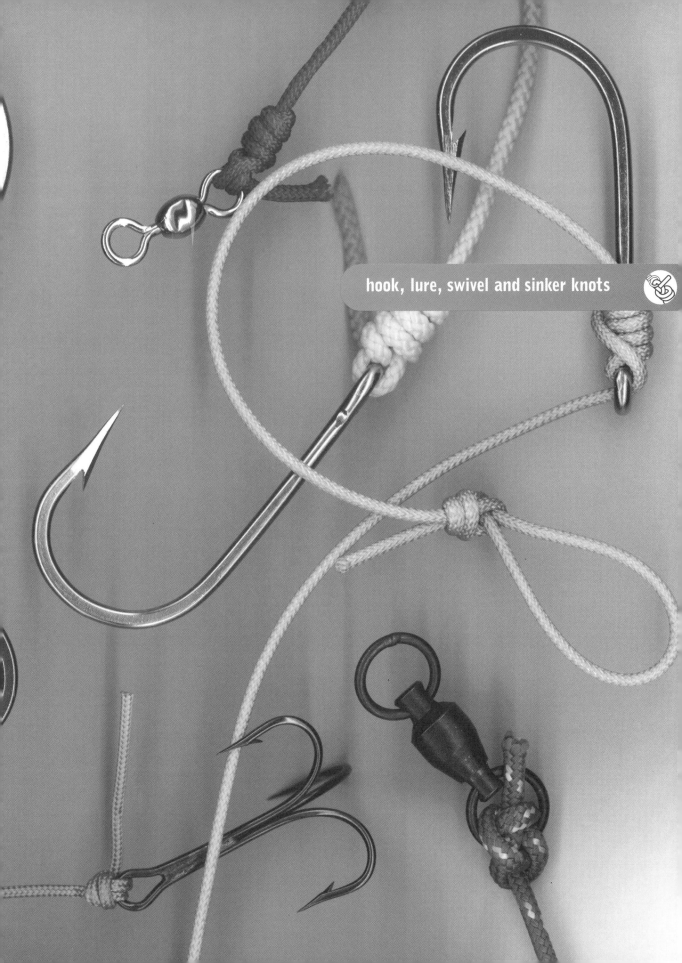

FIGURE OF EIGHT KNOT

APPLICATIONS

A very basic knot, with only four crossing points to generate friction and spread the load, this classic horsehair and gut fastening – which is no longer effective in monofilament – is still used for braided wire (coated or uncoated).

METHOD

Tie as shown. Pull on the tag end to remove all possible slack from the knot, then push the collar that encircles the standing part of the line towards the eye or ring to trap it (figs. 1-2).

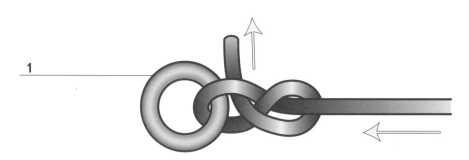

1

2

HISTORY

The American knotsman Clifford Ashley claimed that his ex-school friend Chippet, a contortionist with Barnum & Bailey's circus, could tie himself in a figure of eight knot. So can the developing *Leucothris mucor*, a colourless, macroscopic, filamentous marine bacterium of the algae family. The Incas of Peru used it in their decimalized accounting cords called quipus. The name 'figure of eight' knot surfaces first in Darcy Lever's 1808 seamanship manual, the *Young Officer's Sheet Anchor*, prior to which it was more commonly referred to as the Flemish knot.

<96>

CRAWFORD KNOT

APPLICATIONS

This established knot (it has existed with this name for at least twenty-five years) is readily tied. Although fairly basic, its ten crossing points make it stronger and more secure than the preceding figure of eight knot.

METHOD

Wrap and tuck as shown (figs. 1-2). Pull first on the tag end to tighten the knot, then upon the standing part of the line to slide the knot towards the hook (fig. 3) and close down the loop.

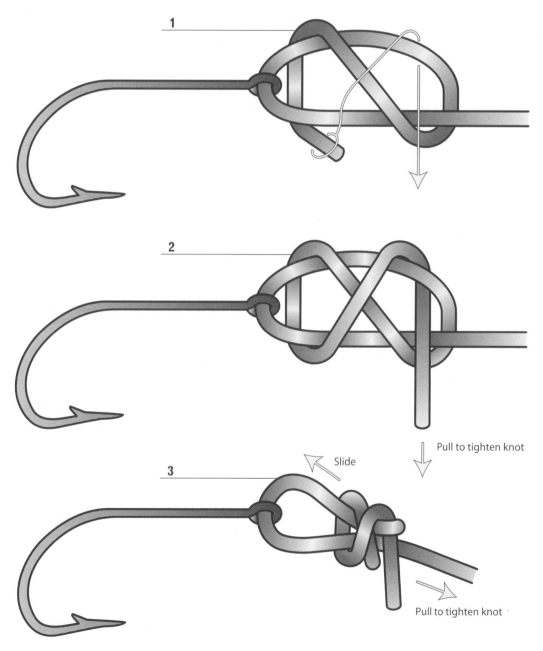

1

2

Pull to tighten knot

3

Slide

Pull to tighten knot

<97>

SWIVEL KNOT

APPLICATIONS

This is a quick and easy attachment for swivels, although its simplicity renders it less secure than other more elaborate knots.

METHOD

Pass the working end up through the ring of the swivel, then around first the neck of the hardware and then the standing part of the line, in a figure of eight layout (fig. 1). Tuck and trap the tag end beneath the initial loop (fig. 2) and pull the entire knot snug and tight around the neck of the swivel (fig. 3).

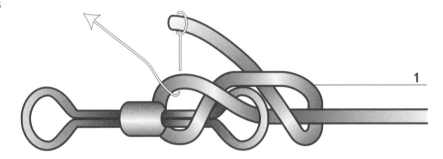

1

2

3

HISTORY

This is a bag or sack binding knot which – since the demise of granaries and dry goods stores, in an age of pre-packaged merchandise – has found alternative employment as a fishing knot beside or afloat on river, lake, gravel pit, reservoir and sea. It can be found listed as a fishing knot in 50-year-old knot manuals.

<98>

CAIRNTON KNOT

APPLICATIONS

Yet another survivor from the days of gut and horsehair angling, this method of attaching the line to a fly is one of several knots that are seized to the shank and contrive a straight (albeit offset) pull through an angled eye.

METHOD

Pass the working end through the eye, then wrap and tuck it as shown (figs. 1-2). Tighten so that it beds down snugly beside the eye (fig. 3).

HISTORY

W.A. Hunter published this knot in his 1927 book *Fisherman's Knots and Wrinkles*, having had it sent to him from a place called Cairnton by Mr. A.H.E. Woods — hence its other name, the Woods knot.

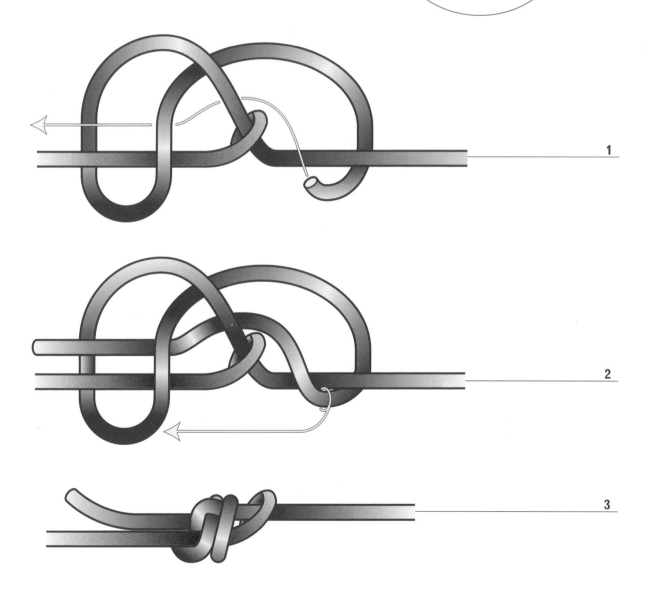

1

2

3

<99>

CLINCH KNOT

APPLICATIONS

The clinch knot is a pure angling knot, with no known applications elsewhere. It is also called a half blood knot or stevedore knot (not to be confused with the real stevedore knot used by dock workers working with rope hoists and tackles). Expert opinion is divided over whether or not this strong (95%) knot is suitable for heavy lines in which it can prove difficult to tighten. Try it in thicker monofilaments with just three or four turns, rather than the five customary for thinner ones. In the lightest lines, tie the knot with the line doubled.

METHOD 1

Pass the working end through the eye or ring and take 3½ wraps around the standing part of the line. Bring the end back through and tuck it through the loop beside the point of attachment (fig. 1) and flype the knot (pull it inside out) to form a half blood knot (fig. 2). Finally tighten it snugly against the eye or ring (fig. 3).

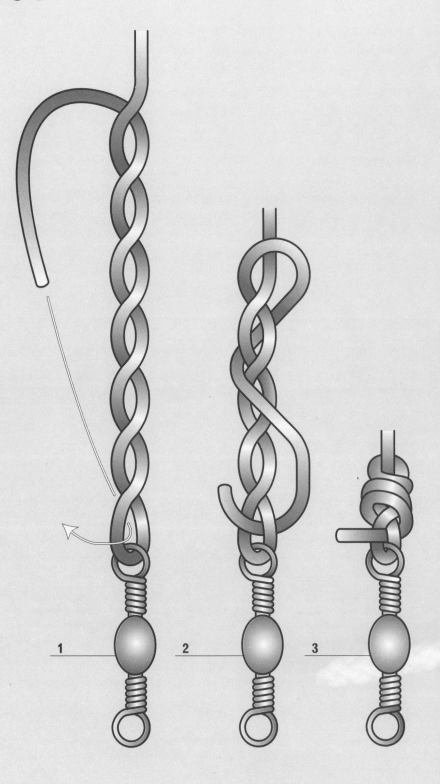

1

2

3

<100>

METHOD 2

Having begun method 1 (see method 1 – fig. 1), whether in single or doubled line, tuck the working end a second time as shown (figs. 1-2). As well as making the knot more secure, this extra tuck may also add a few percentage points to the strength of the knot.

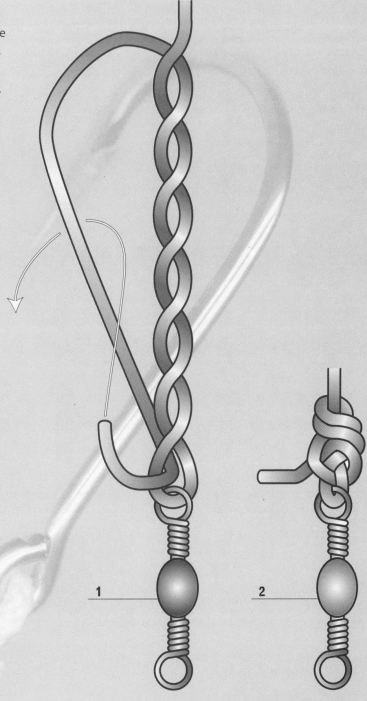

1

2

<101>

TRILENE KNOT

APPLICATIONS

Hook knots are stronger when the line has been passed twice through the eye of the hook, where the size of both eye and line allow the modification. This is one of several such knots. Like the preceding clinch knot, it can be troublesome to tighten in lines over about 5.5kg (12lbs). Still, it is a popular knot.

METHOD

Take a round turn through the eye or ring and then wrap the working end four or five times around the standing part of the line. Bring the end back and tuck it through the round turn (fig. 1). Pull, push and generally knead the knot into a blood knot form before tightening it (figs. 2-3).

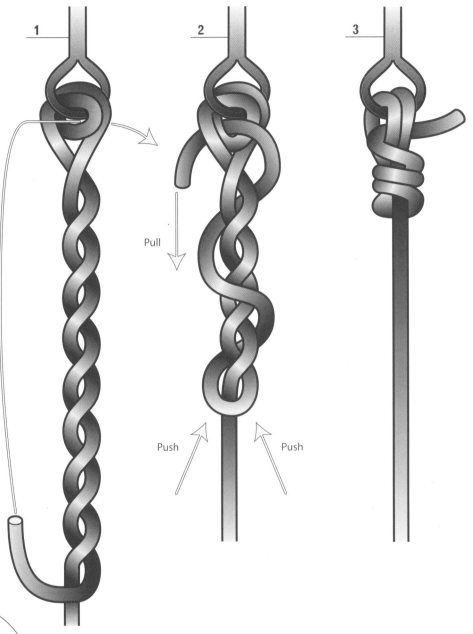

1

2

Pull

Push   Push

3

HISTORY

This knot is also known as the Berkley Trilene knot, implying an origin in an eponymous trade publication or for use with that particular brand of tackle.

<102>

ANCHOR BEND (VARIANT)

APPLICATIONS

Use this knot when you want to tie hooks, lures or flies to lines or leaders.

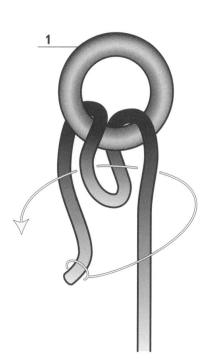

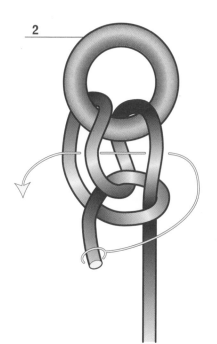

METHOD

Take a round turn through the eye or ring (fig. 1). Then pass the working end through it twice, wrapping towards the point of attachment, and tighten the knot (figs. 2-3). It is sometimes suggested that a third tuck (not illustrated) should be added in super braids; but, in such cases, this is perhaps the wrong knot for the job and a suitable alternative (see the Jansik special that comes next) may be preferable.

HISTORY

This knot appeared recently in *The Little Red Fishing Knot Book* by Harry Nilsson, where it is labelled Harry's knot (implying another of those genuine periodic re-discoveries). But it is far from original, even as an angling knot. It featured in W.A. Hunter's *Fisherman's Knots and Wrinkles* (1927) as an attachment for a swivel. It was also a means of bending an underwater warp (rope) to an anchor, appearing in an anonymous 1904 manual of seamanship.

<103>

JANSIK SPECIAL

APPLICATIONS

Another knot with two line parts through an eye or ring, this knot has tested 100% efficient in terms of breaking strength on a hook, swivel or lure, using light monofilaments. Try it also as an alternative to the preceding anchor bend variant.

METHOD

Pass the working end of the line twice through the ring or eye – in other words, take a round turn – then make three wrapping turns to enclose three inert knot parts as shown (figs. 1-2). Pull the knot tight, ensuring that an even load will fall upon each one of the loops through the ring or eye (fig. 3).

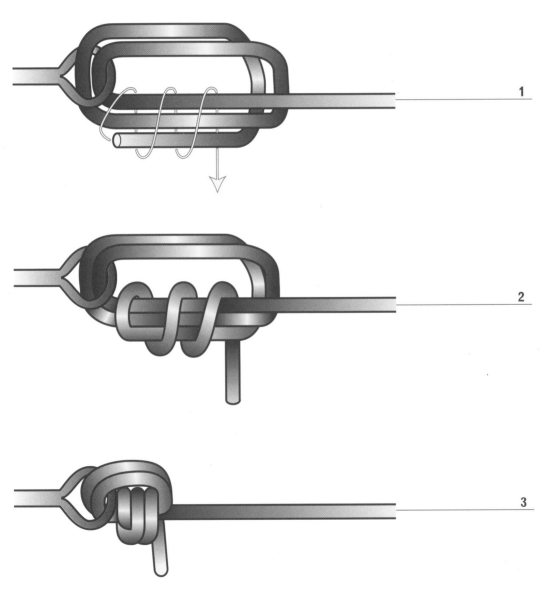

1

2

3

<104>

PALOMAR KNOT

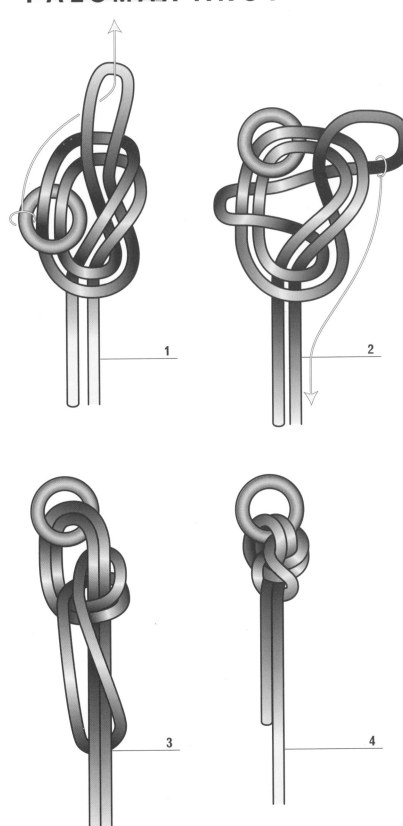

1

2

3

4

APPLICATIONS

A loop or bight of line is another way to double the hold upon a ring or eye. As the hook or lure must – in this instance – be passed through the loop of the half-completed knot, this may be impractical with any multiple hook or other complicated tackle rig. Similarly, if tied in a doubled fly fishing line (rather than an existing long loop), it shortens the tapered leader. Nonetheless, it is a fairly strong and very secure knot, easily learnt and tied, which may even be used around reels as an arbor knot (see Other Useful Knots).

METHOD

Insert a long-ish loop (long enough to pass over the hook or lure) through the ring or eye and tie an overhand knot (fig. 1). Tuck the hook through the loop (fig. 2), then bring the loop back over the half-form knot to form a collar around the standing part of the doubled line (fig. 3) and tighten the knot (fig. 4).

HISTORY

The origins of this knot are unknown to me, other than to remark that there is a Mount Palomar in California, the site of an astronomical observatory.

<105>

WORLD'S FAIR KNOT

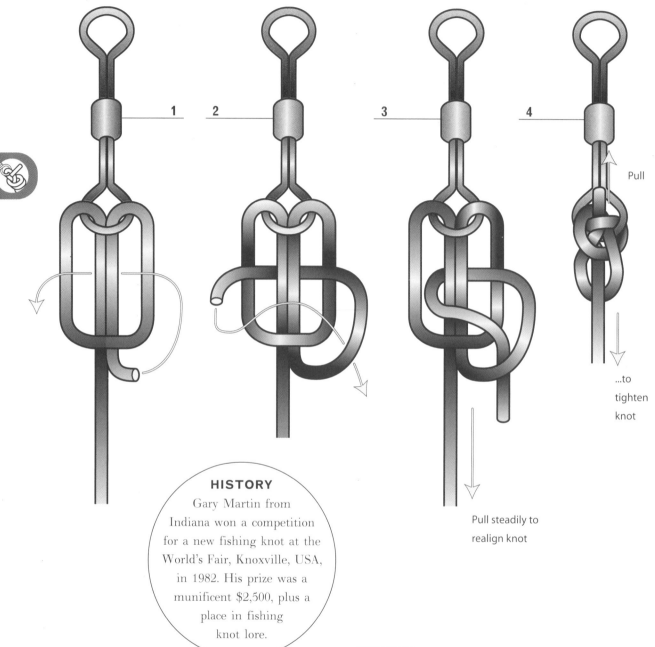

1 2 3 4

Pull

...to tighten knot

Pull steadily to realign knot

APPLICATIONS

This 17-year-old knot secures line to hook to other terminal tackle by means of a loop or long bight of doubled line, but (unlike the Palomar knot) does not require to have a hook or other item of hardware tucked through it.

METHOD

Pass a loop through the ring or eye and double it over to lay upon both inert standing parts. Take the working end and make a locking tuck, going under/over(two parts)/under (fig. 1), then finally tuck the tag end back beneath its own standing part (fig. 2). Pull the tag end and standing part in opposite directions to realign this knot and tighten it (figs. 3-4).

<106>

CAT'S PAW

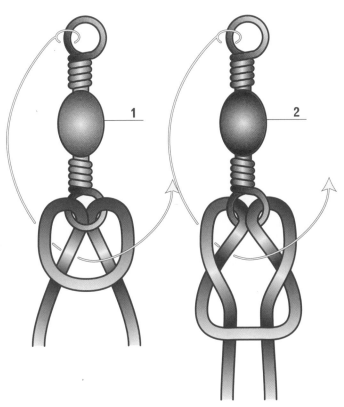

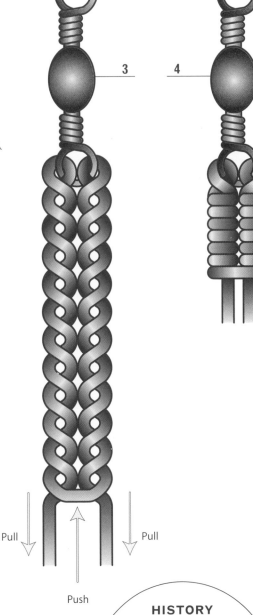

1

2

3

4

Pull

Push

Pull

APPLICATIONS

This strong ring hitch attaches the loop of a Bimini twist or similar long loop to a swivel or a hook, primarily for offshore big game fishing.

METHOD

Pass the end of a loop through ring or eye and double it back on itself (fig. 1). Next tuck the hook or swivel, in a succession of backward somersaults (a total of seven to ten), through the space between both inert loop legs and the loop itself (fig. 2). There should then be an identical number of twists on each side of the knot, one set spiralling left-handed or clockwise, the others right-handed or anti(counter)-clockwise. Pull on both loop legs, straightening them (fig. 3), and then slide the wrapping turns that result close together alongside the point of attachment (fig. 4).

HISTORY

The angling alias for this knot is the offshore knot but its older nautical name – cat's paw (from a 1794 seamanship manual) – has been in continuous use for 200 years.

<107>

TURLE KNOT

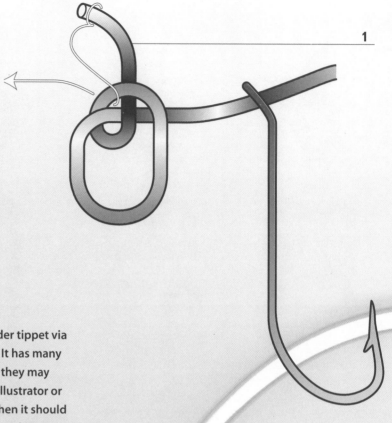

1

APPLICATIONS

This knot is designed to attach fly to leader tippet via a hook eye that turns either up or down. It has many variations, some of dubious origin, since they may have arisen merely because some book illustrator or knot tyer mistakenly drew a tuck over when it should have gone under. Only three, time-honoured methods are described and illustrated.

METHOD 1 (BASIC KNOT)

Pass the working end of the line through the eye of the hook and then make a 360 degree loop by tying it around the standing part of the line (figs. 1-2). Whatever the handedness of the knot (left-handed in the specimen shown), ensure that the belly of the knot encloses the knot in such a way that it is skewed (see Fundamental Knots on page 35). Pull the hook through the loop. The knot can be tightened around the shank of the hook to lie snugly alongside the angled eye (fig. 3). A tag end that projects from its knot more or less at right-angles, causing vibration in the water, may be a desirable feature in a lure; but, if not, tuck it instead so as to lie alongside the shank in the tightened knot (figs. 4-5).

<108>

2 _____

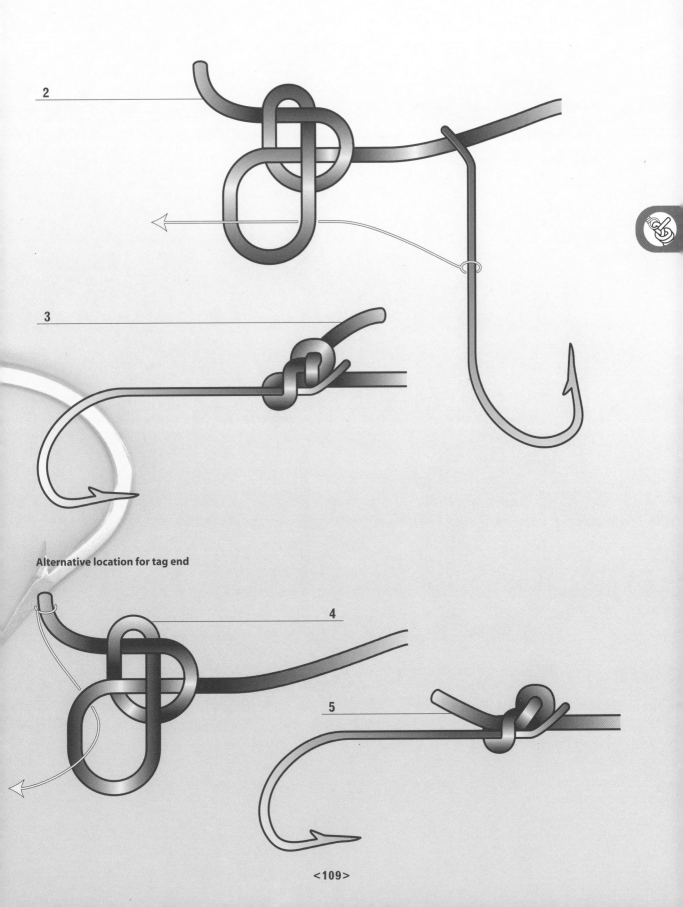

3 _____

Alternative location for tag end

4 _____

5 _____

<109>

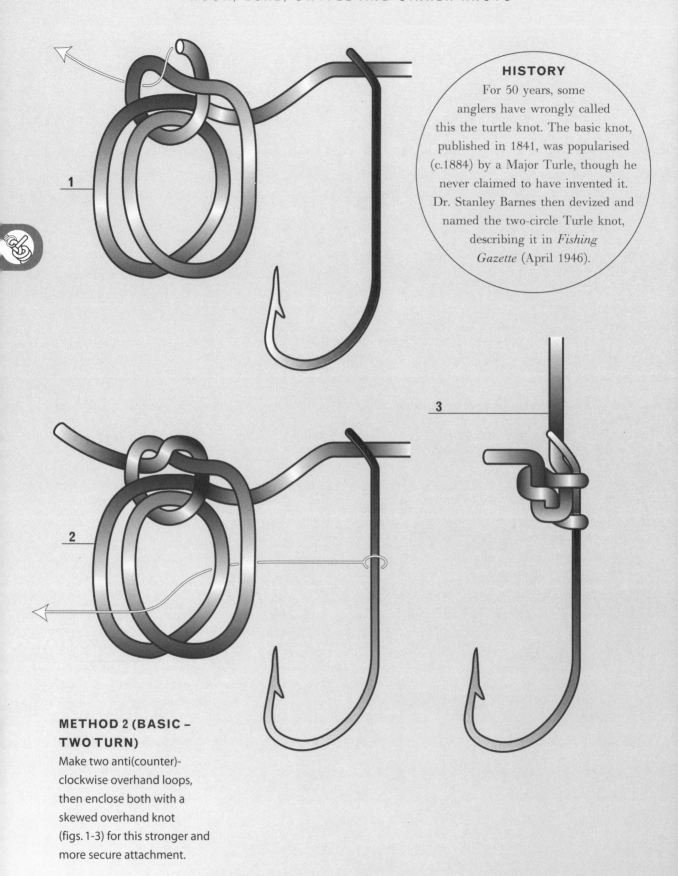

HISTORY

For 50 years, some anglers have wrongly called this the turtle knot. The basic knot, published in 1841, was popularised (c.1884) by a Major Turle, though he never claimed to have invented it. Dr. Stanley Barnes then devized and named the two-circle Turle knot, describing it in *Fishing Gazette* (April 1946).

1

3

2

METHOD 2 (BASIC – TWO TURN)

Make two anti(counter)-clockwise overhand loops, then enclose both with a skewed overhand knot (figs. 1-3) for this stronger and more secure attachment.

<110>

METHOD 3 (SECURED BASIC AND TWO TURN VERSIONS)

Improved security of the basic Turle knot in synthetic lines has been achieved by tucking the tag end a second time through the overhand knot (figs. 1-2). The two-turn version can be similarly modified (fig. 3).

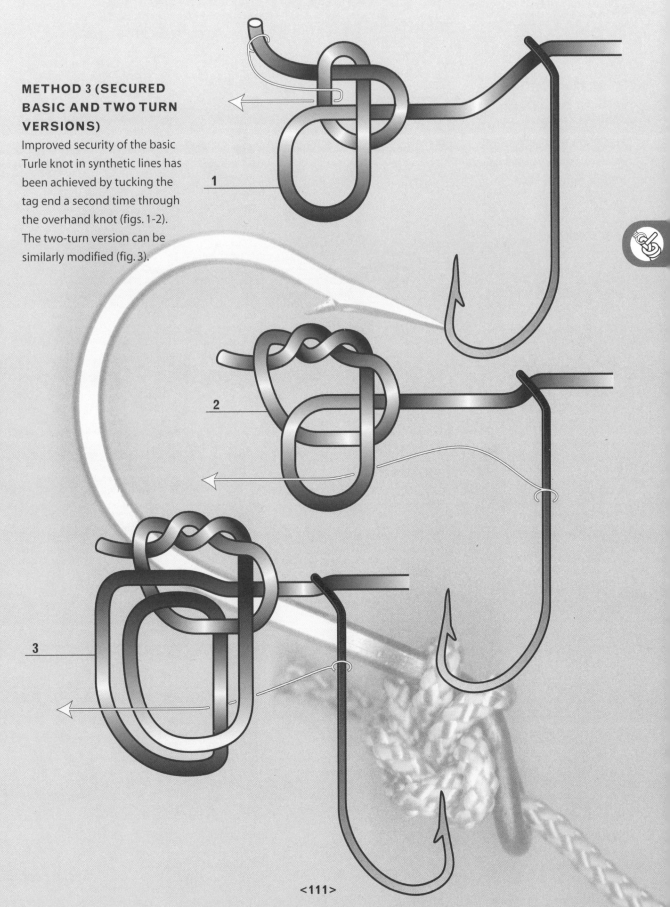

1

2

3

<111>

DRY FLY KNOT

APPLICATIONS

This is one of the best knots for attaching any fly (dry or otherwise) – with a hook eye turned up or down – to a leader tippet.

METHOD

Pass the working end through the eye and take a turn with it around the standing part of the line. Take a second turn around the line, overlapping the first one (fig. 1). Then tuck the working end twice through and around the two loops already formed (fig. 2), before pulling upon the standing part and sliding the two turns in the opposite direction over the eye to surround the shank of the fly hook (fig. 3). Now tighten the knot (fig. 4).

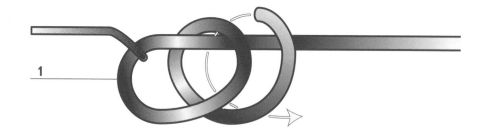

1

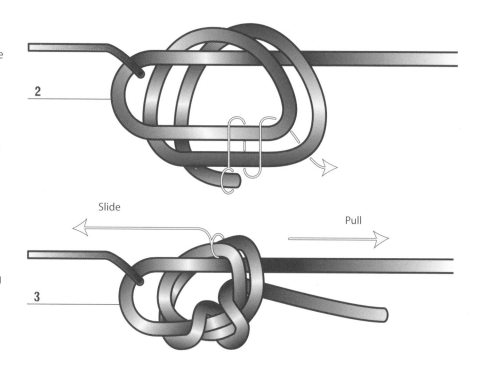

2

Slide   Pull

3

4

HISTORY

George Harvey of Penn State University, USA, is credited with pioneering this knot.

<112>

LOOP KNOT

APPLICATIONS
This fairly strong and versatile knot is simple enough to tie by feel in poor light.

METHOD
Tuck the loop of a simple noose through the ring or eye and then pass the hook, swivel or whatever through the loop (fig. 1). Finally trap the tag end within the loop (figs. 2-3) and tighten the knot (fig. 4).

HISTORY
The Australian fishing writer Frank Marshall is credited with having introduced this knot to his angling readers some decades ago and so it is known to them as the Marshall snare knot, whereas 1990s American angling writer Bob McNally calls it the double eye knot.

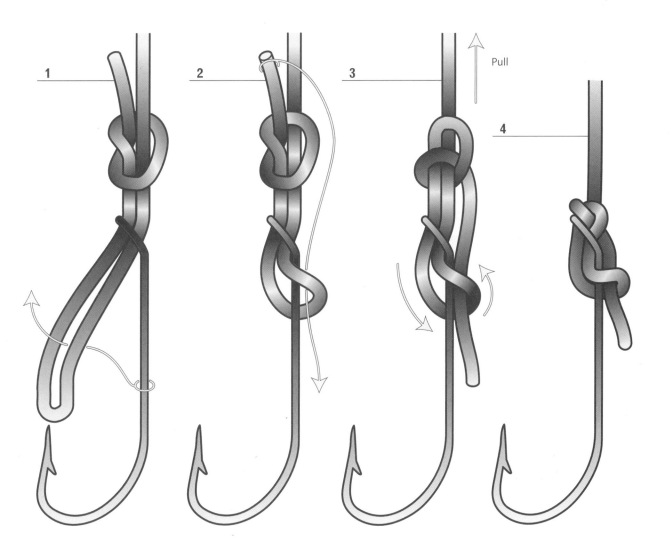

1

2

3

Pull

4

<113>

TANDEM HOOK KNOT

APPLICATIONS
When a second hook is to be added in line with another one, some kind of tandem rig is required. The intermediate knot required, of which this is an example, can be somewhat simpler than the one at the end of the line.

METHOD
Insert the line through the eye of the hook to be secured and merely tie a double overhand knot around the shank (fig. 1), while leaving a sufficiently long end for the other hook (fig. 2).

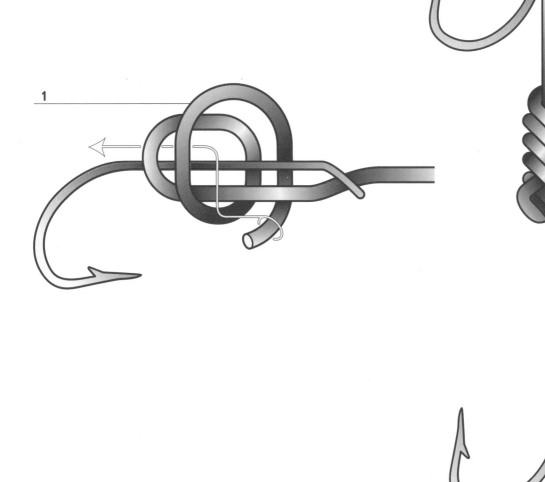

<114>

KNOTLESS KNOT

APPLICATIONS

This is an alternative to the tandem hook knot on the previous page for fixing a hook so as to leave the end of line free for some other attachment.

METHOD

Lay the line alongside the shank of the hook, pass the working end through the eye, and make four or five wrapping turns to enclose both shank and line (fig. 1). Pass the end back over these turns and through the eye once again (fig. 2), then pull the knot tightly snug beside the eye (fig. 3).

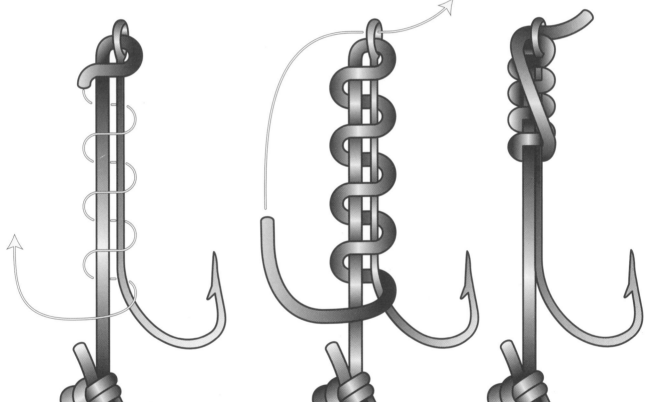

1   2   3

<115>

SIMPLE SNELL

APPLICATIONS

This simplified version of snelling is weaker and less secure than the full version (which follows) but it is more quickly and easily tied.

METHOD

Pass the working end through the eye and lay the line along the shank of the hook, prior to taking four or five wrapping tucks (in the direction of the eye) with the end around both shank and line (figs. 1-2). Finally tuck the tag end down between the shank and line and tighten the knot (fig. 3).

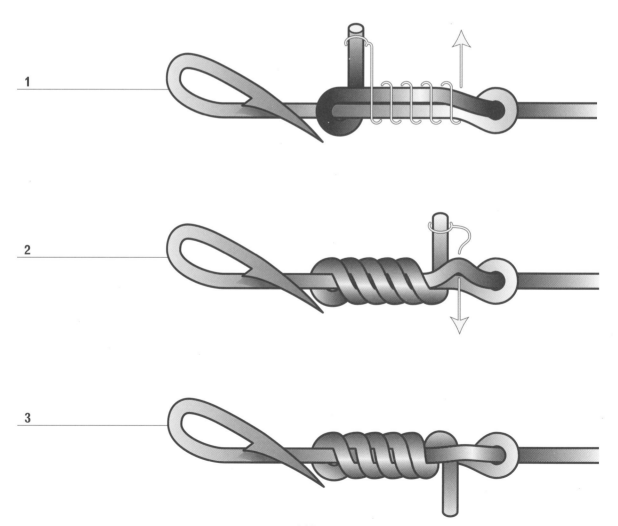

1

2

3

<116>

SNELLING

APPLICATIONS
The snell is an extremely strong connection from line to hook shank – well tied it has tested 100%.

METHOD
Pass the working end through the eye of the hook, then form an anti(counter)-clockwise overhand loop, before wrapping and tucking to enclose the inert standing part of the line along the shank of the hook (fig. 1). Carefully flype (peel inside out) this arrangement into the familiar barrel-shaped blood knot (fig. 2) and tighten (fig. 3).

HISTORY
The word 'snelling' seems to have come from the professional sea-fishermen, known as long-liners, who work with a large number of anchored and connected baited hooks. It has now been adopted by sport anglers.

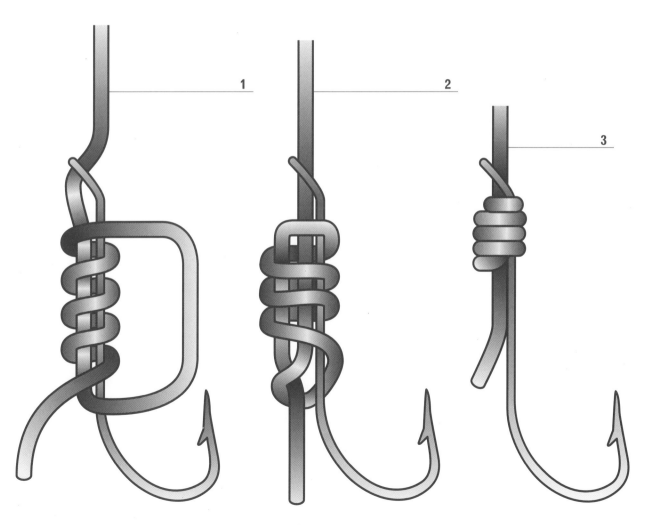

<117>

DOMHOF KNOT

APPLICATIONS

Use this as an alternative to snelling around the shank of a hook, when flyping wrapped turns into a blood knot will not work. It is another example of the 'trombone' type of knot (see trombone loop on page 62).

METHOD

Pass the end of a line through an angled (up or down) hook eye and bring it back to create a trombone loop (fig. 1). Enclose both loop legs together with the hook shank in a series of neatly bedded wrapping turns (fig. 2). Finally tuck the end through what remains of the loop (fig. 3) and pull upon the standing part of the line to tighten the knot and trap the tag end (fig. 4).

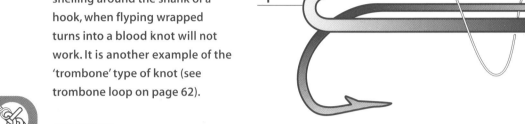

1

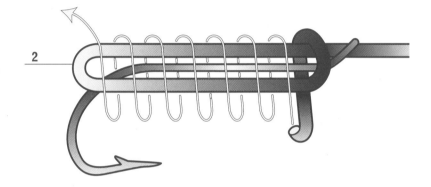

2

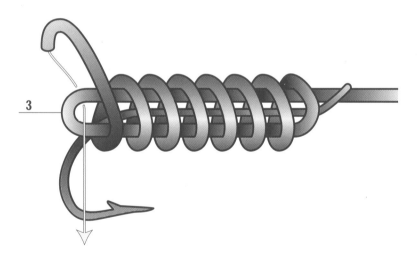

3

4

Pull to tighten knot

HISTORY

This knot has also appeared as the sliding bait loop (in Canada) and as the spade end knot and – confusingly – trombone loop (in the UK).

<118>

LOCK KNOT

APPLICATIONS

Many shank seizings are only intended for up-turned or down-turned eyes, but this one is said to have been designed especially for attaching monofilament to flat eyed hooks.

METHOD

Lay the line alongside the shank of the hook and wrap it around once before bringing the end back and down through the eye. Wrap the working end four times to enclose the shank and two line parts (fig. 1), then tuck the tag end up through the bight (fig. 2). Pull on the standing part of the line, ensuring that all the turns bed down snugly before sliding the knot up against the eye (figs. 3-4).

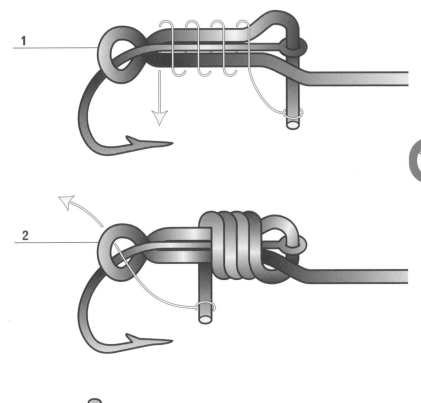

1

2

3

Pull to tighten knot

HISTORY

This knot is reported to have originated in France where it is called the serrure knot ('serrure' translates as 'lock').

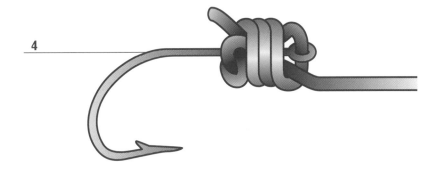

4

<119>

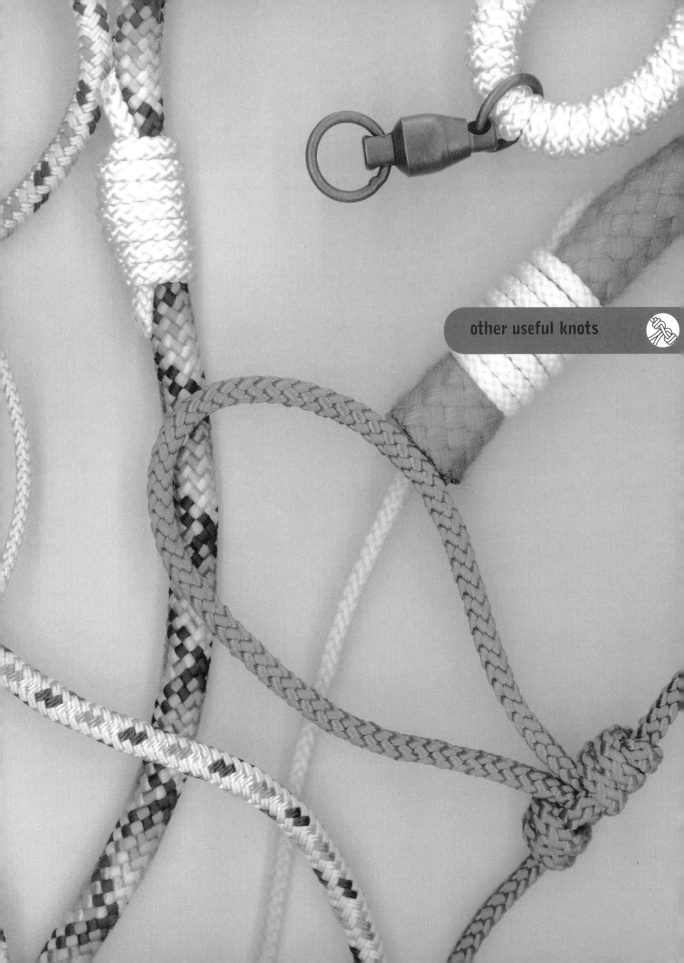

ARBOR KNOTS

APPLICATIONS
Any sliding loop that attaches a line to the spindle (arbor) of a reel may be called an arbor knot. It should not be bulky, and need be only moderately secure since no backing line should ever be so fully extended as to rely solely upon this knot.

METHOD 1 (DOUBLE OVERHAND KNOT)
Cast an anti(counter)-clockwise underhand loop and tie the working end to the standing part of the line with a double overhand knot (figs. 1-2). This arrangement will encircle and grip the round cross-section of any reel.

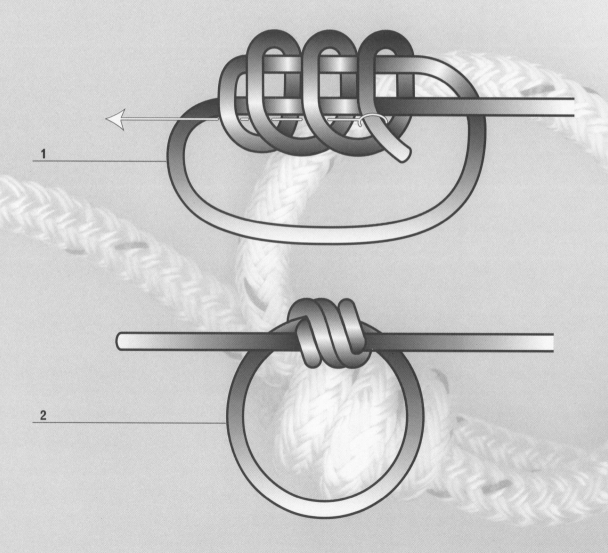

<122>

METHOD 2 (SIMPLE SIMON)

This is easier to tie because it lacks the final awkward tuck of the preceding knot. Cast an anti(counter)-clockwise underhand loop as before, but this time follow a figure of eight layout before making the locking tuck (fig. 1). Tighten the knot (fig. 2).

1

2

<123>

BLOOD KNOT LOOP

APPLICATIONS

Use this to create a loop in thinner line, which is then attached to a thicker backing line.

METHOD

Double or middle a length of line to make a bight and wrap the working end of another line at least three times around both legs of the initial bight before tucking it as shown (fig. 1). Then similarly wrap and tuck the twin ends of the loop line to complete this compound knot (fig. 2). Pull it tight (fig. 3).

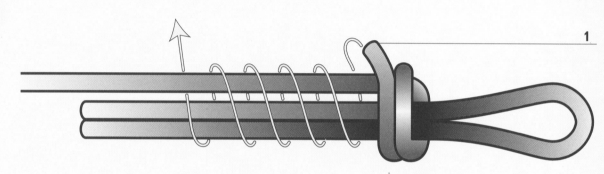

1

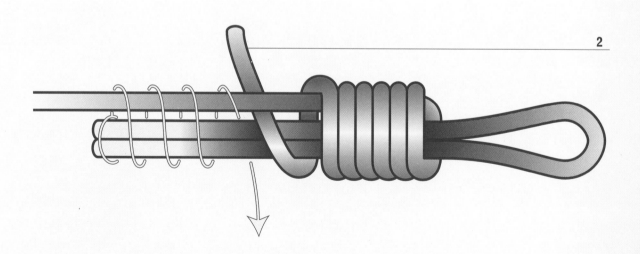

2

<124>

HISTORY
Stanley Barnes, M.D., D.Sc.,
LL.D., F.R.C.P., formerly Dean of
the Faculty of Medicine at the
University of Birmingham, England,
illustrated and described this ingenious
loop knot in his book *Anglers' Knots in
Gut and Nylon* (1948). It is another knot
that has made the transition from
natural fibre fishing lines
to prove effective in
synthetic materials.

3

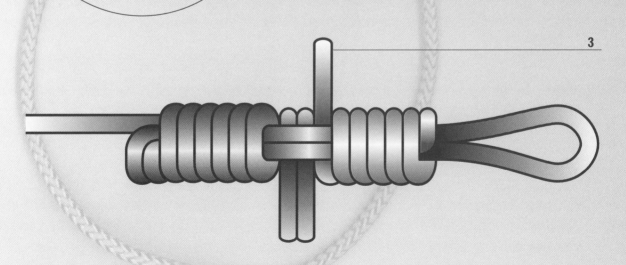

<125>

BLOOD LOOP DROPPER KNOTS

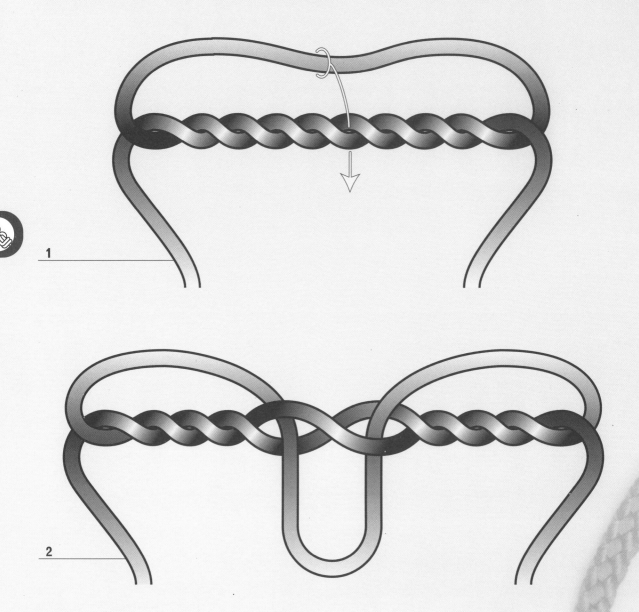

1

2

APPLICATIONS

A dropper knot makes a loop that stands out at right-angles to a fishing line for the attachment of extra flies (droppers) in fly fishing. Also, when fishing from beach or boat, it enables additional hooks or sinkers (weights) to make up a paternoster system.

METHOD 1

It is a fact that many loop knots make sound joining knots if the loop is cut off (and vice versa). It follows that a blood loop dropper knot can be tied in the standing part of a single length of line. To do so, tie a multiple overhand knot, locate the middle of the entwined knot parts, and pull the large bight or belly of the knot down through it to form a bight (figs. 1-2). Draw the knot into a snug blood or barrel-shaped form (fig. 3).

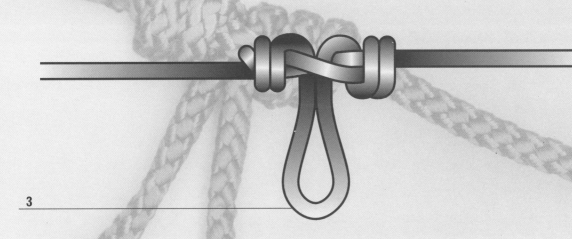

3

METHOD 2

Tuck both working ends of a blood knot in the same direction and then knot them to create a strong dropper loop (fig. 1).

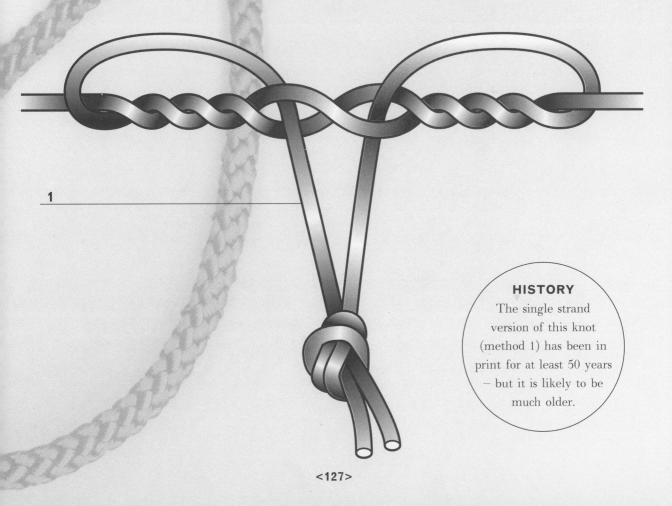

1

<127>

ALPINE BUTTERFLY

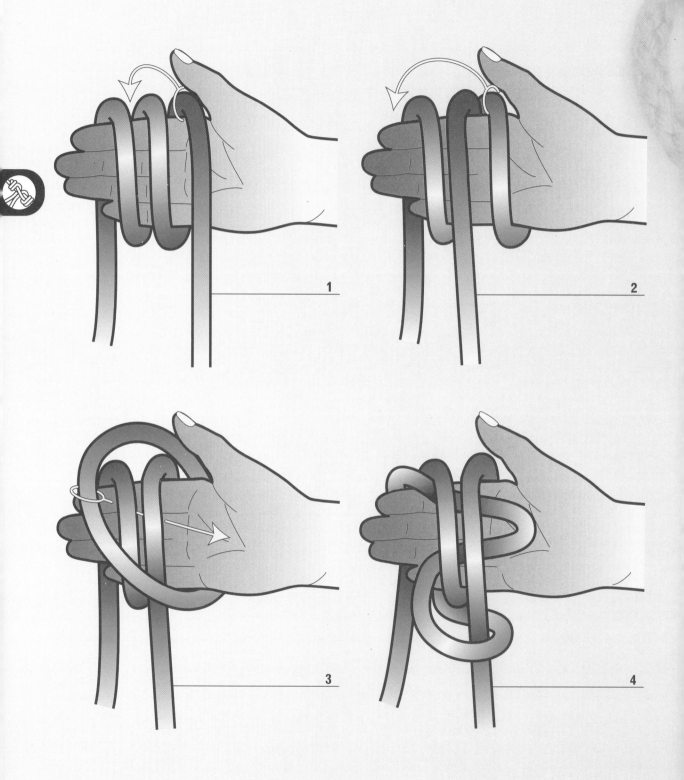

<128>

APPLICATIONS

Try this knot as an alternative dropper loop.

METHOD

There are a number of ways to tie the Alpine butterfly, each of which has its adherents. I like the easily learnt leap-frog routine of the following method. Take two turns around a hand. Then lift the right-hand part to the middle (fig. 1) and the new right-hand part over to the left-hand side (fig. 2). Now pull the resulting bight through the middle of both round turns from right to left (figs. 3-4). Tighten the knot (figs. 5-6). Right-handers may wish to reverse these instructions.

HISTORY

The Alpine butterfly is a classic climbing knot, popular with mountaineers and cavers because the loop can be pulled in several directions at once without capsizing it. It may appeal to anglers for the same reason. After A.P. (Sir Alan) Herbert (1890-1971) wrote a poem, the first line of which was "The bowline is the King of knots", John Sweet responded in *Scout Pioneering* (1974) that ". . . the Alpine butterfly must surely be the Queen".

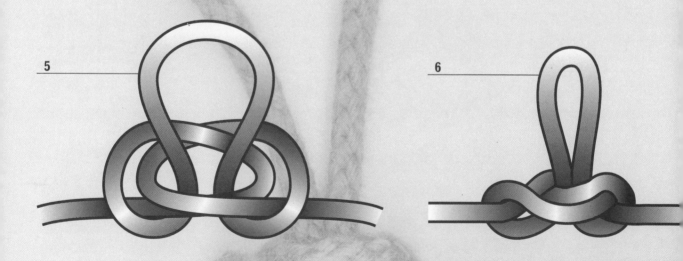

5

6

<129>

LINFIT LOOP

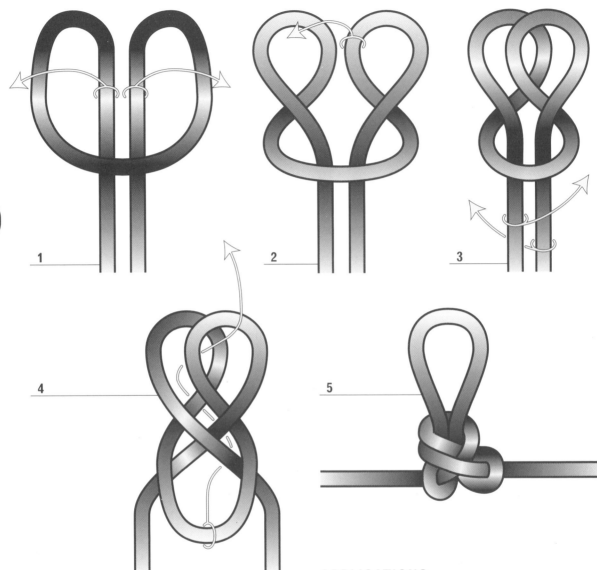

APPLICATIONS

This comparative newcomer to the angling scene has proved itself a robust alternative to the blood loop dropper and the Alpine butterfly.

METHOD

Take a large bight of line and bend it forward and down to create twin loops (fig. 1). Impart matching half twists to each of these loops (fig. 2) and overlap them, right over left (fig. 3). Then pull the bight up through both loops - from back to front, as shown (fig. 4) – and draw everything snug and tight (fig. 5).

HISTORY

This is another knot from the inventive fingers of fisherman Owen K. Nuttall[IGKT] of Linthwaite, Huddersfield, England. It appeared in *Knotting Matters* in October 1986.

<130>

OVERHAND DROPPER KNOT

APPLICATIONS

This secure alternative to a blood dropper loop, an Alpine butterfly, or the Linfit knot, is simpler to tie. Use it to attach two flies at once.

METHOD

Into an overhand knot tied in the main line insert a short dropper length. Take it up through the common space between the two entwined parts of the knot, around the belly, then back down through again to emerge where it entered (figs. 1-2). Tighten (fig. 3). If only one hook or lure is attached, securely tie the free end to prevent it sliding out of the overhand knot.

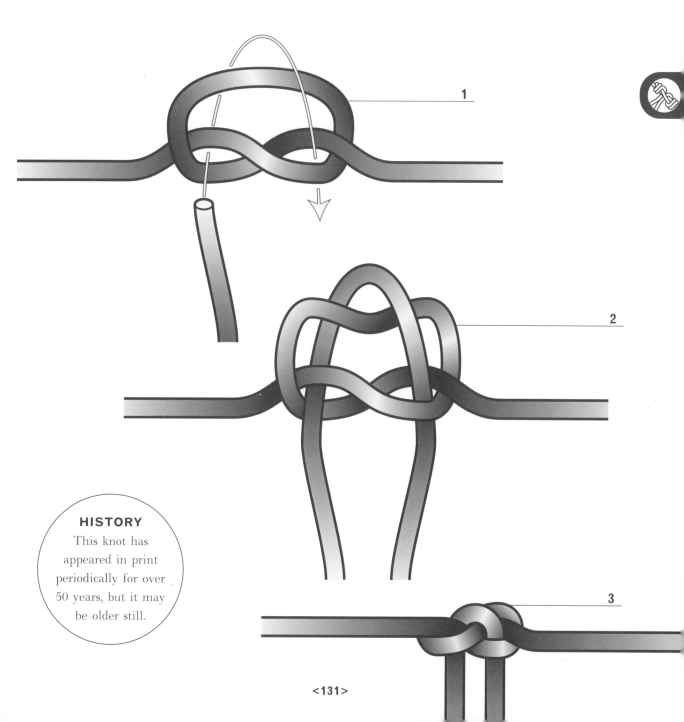

1

2

HISTORY

This knot has appeared in print periodically for over 50 years, but it may be older still.

3

<131>

STOP KNOTS

APPLICATIONS

As a strike indicator, depth marker, or physical stop, a variety of simple knots can be embellished or augmented with bits of coloured wool, strips of cloth or other highly visible fragments of material.

METHOD 1 (FIXED)

Tie a clove hitch in the bight by the direct method of casting two anti(counter)-clockwise loops, overlapping them, and then tucking an elastic band through before tightening the knot around it (figs. 1-3).

METHOD 2 (SLIDING)

Pull a bight of line through an elastic band or ring of some other suitable endless band (fig. 1) and then tuck the working end through the bight (fig. 2) to make a crossing knot. Pull the line out straight (fig. 3) to convert the marker into a figure of eight layout.

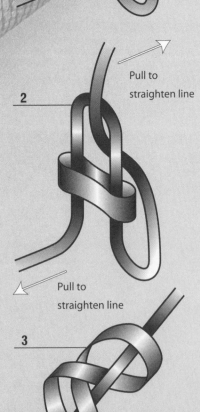

1

1

2

Pull to straighten line

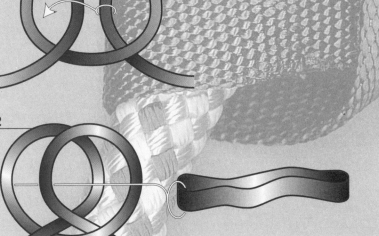

2

Pull to straighten line

3

3

<132>

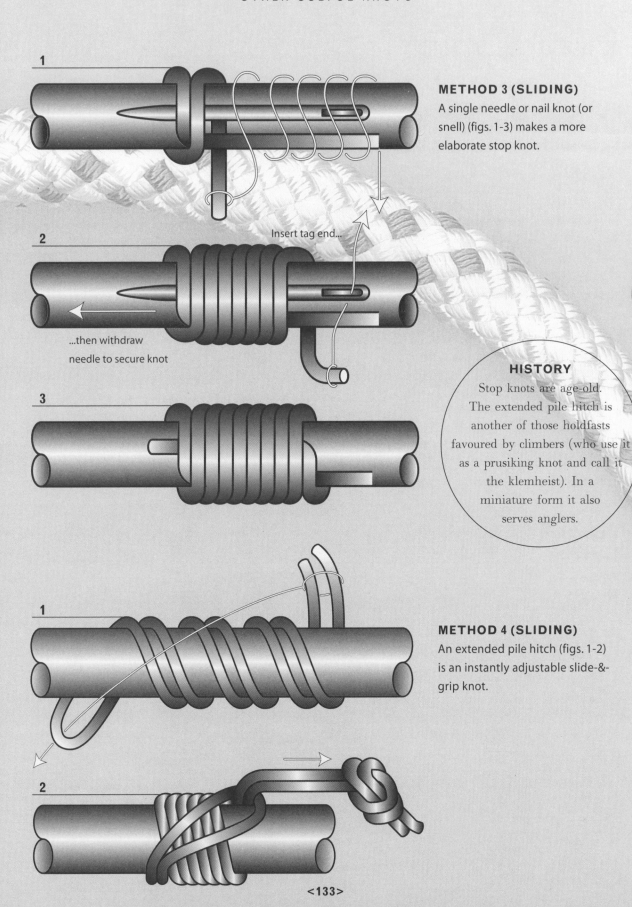

1

METHOD 3 (SLIDING)
A single needle or nail knot (or snell) (figs. 1-3) makes a more elaborate stop knot.

Insert tag end...

2

...then withdraw needle to secure knot

3

1

METHOD 4 (SLIDING)
An extended pile hitch (figs. 1-2) is an instantly adjustable slide-&-grip knot.

2

<133>

NEEDLE KNOT

APPLICATIONS

The needle knot forms a strong yet streamlined attachment for a monofilament leader to a fly line.

METHOD

Push a needle into the end of the fly line and out through one side (fig. 1). If the hole that is created will not remain open, a gently heated needle may do the trick. Trim or point the working end of the leader by slicing it with a sharp blade at an acute angle and then push the end of the leader through the hole already made by the needle (fig. 2). Lay the needle alongside the fly line, and take five or six wrapping turns with the working end of the leader around the fly line (fig. 3). Thread the working end of the leader through the eye of the needle and pull it beneath the turns to complete the knot (figs. 4-5).

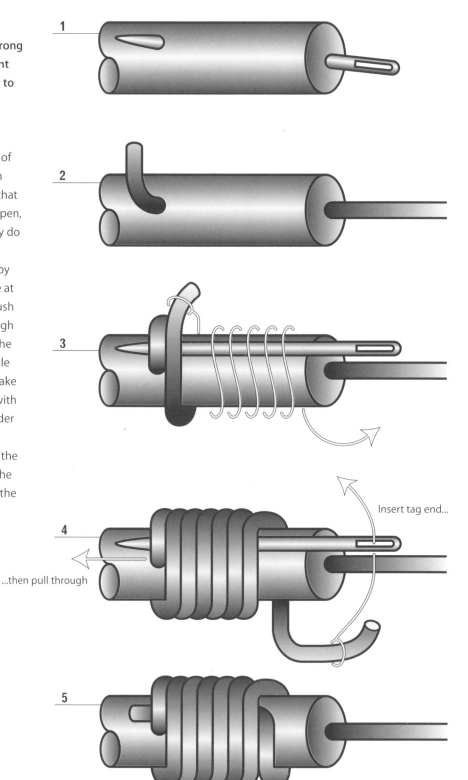

...then pull through

Insert tag end...

<134>

NEEDLE KNOT LOOP

APPLICATIONS

Tie the needle knot loop to facilitate frequent changes of leader on a fly line. It is also referred to as the needle knot (mono loop).

METHOD

Tie this in the same way as the preceding needle knot but using a doubled line instead of a single one (figs. 1-2).

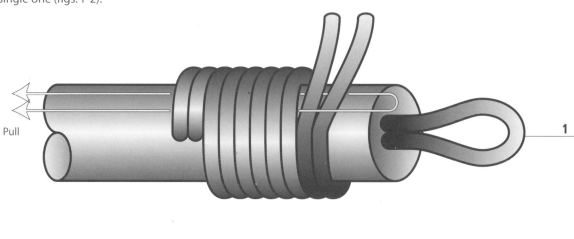

Pull

1

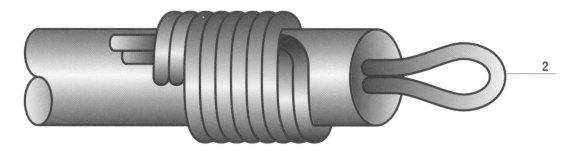

2

<135>

HAYWIRE TWIST

APPLICATIONS

This is the basic strong loop for single-strand wire, either for a stand-alone loop or as an attachment to hook or swivel.

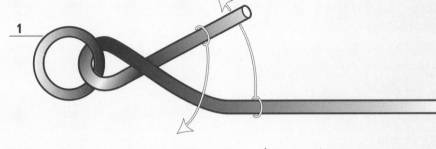

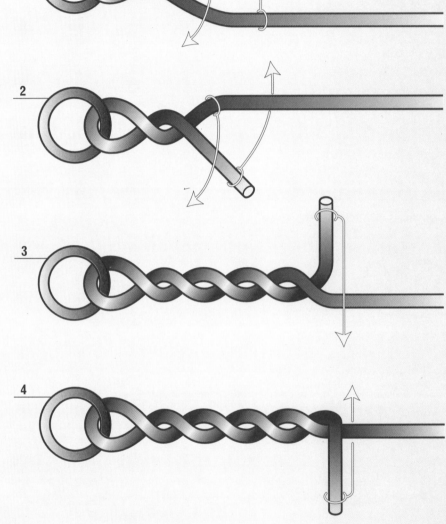

METHOD

Pass the end of the wire through the ring or eye and twist half a turn to make a loop (fig. 1). Make a second half twist to create interlocked elbows (fig. 2). Create at least three or four of these twists – ensuring that both working end and standing part are equally involved (one part must not form a helix while the other remains straight) – and then bend the working end at right angles to the standing part (fig. 3). Bend the end at right-angles, then wrap it around, up and down again, making the first of a series of tight barrel rolls

<136>

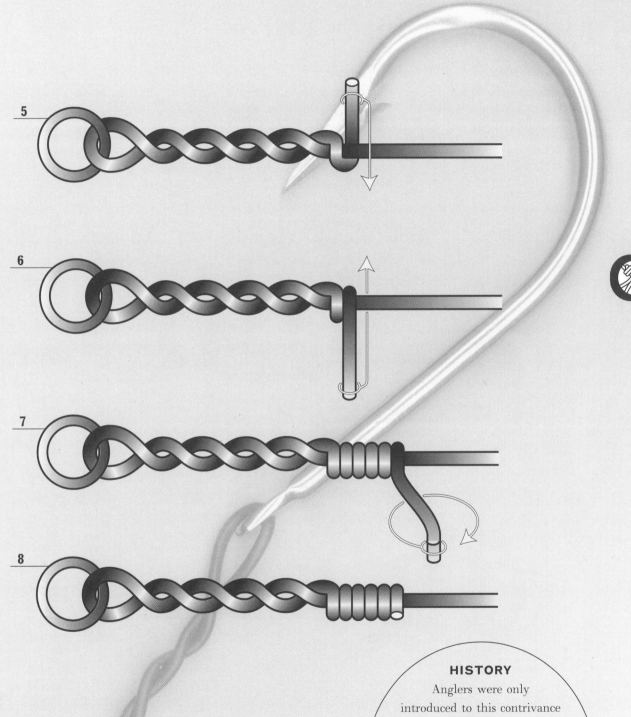

5

6

7

8

(figs. 4-6). Make five or six such wrapping turns, then snap off the end by winding it like a handle until metal fatigue breaks it (fig. 7). The tag end so created should lie flush (and therefore snag-free) with the preceding barrel rolls (fig. 8).

HISTORY

Anglers were only introduced to this contrivance once wire became an established piece of tackle; but drawn wire was invented as long ago as the early fifteenth century and the haywire twist was used by those who first erected wire fences to enclose land and livestock.

<137>

BIG GAME CABLE LOOP

APPLICATIONS

This two-part entwined loop, backed up by a couple of crimps, will give added strength to a cable that must handle marlin, big sharks and other such fish.

METHOD

Select a pair of sleeves of the correct internal diameter and thread them onto the cable before passing its tag end through the swivel ring or hook eye that will be the point of attachment. Leaving a large-ish loop, pass the working end a second time through the ring or eye, then tuck it three times around the loop to tie a triple overhand knot (figs. 1-2).

Now remove slack from the knotting loop, pass the tag end through both sleeves beside its own standing part of the line and neatly crimp both sleeves (using the appropriate tool, obtainable from tackle shops). The sleeves should be about 2.5cm (1in) apart with the one nearest to the knot as close to it as possible (fig. 3).

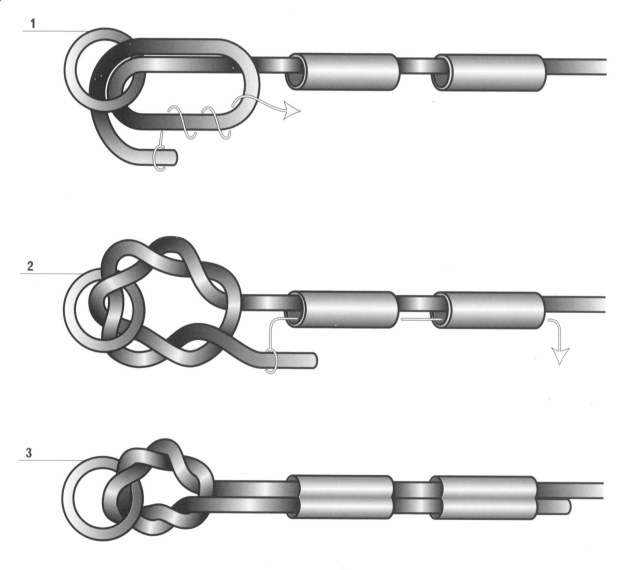

TORUS KNOT

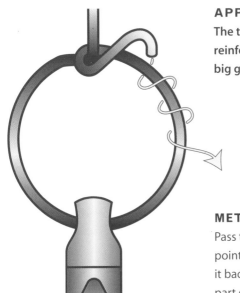

APPLICATIONS

The torus knot is a robust, reinforced loop. Use it for a big game swivel or hook.

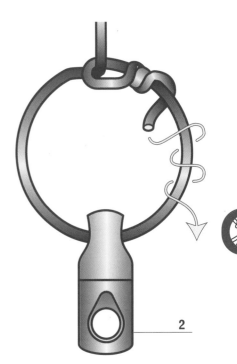

METHOD

Pass the tag end through the point of attachment and bring it back around the standing part of the line (fig. 1) to make a sliding loop. Then wrap the end snugly around the loop in a series of parcelling turns (figs. 2-3) until the entire loop is thus covered. Tuck the tag end and pull the loop tight (fig. 4).

Pull to tighten knot

1

2

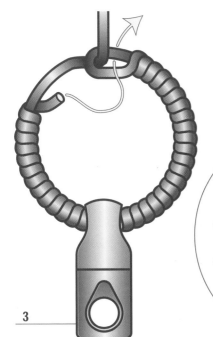

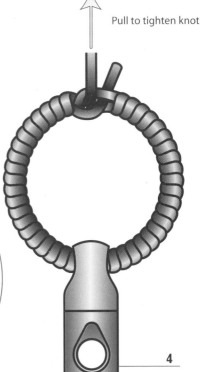

HISTORY

Ropeworkers know this doughnut-shaped ring hitch (the technical name for a ring doughnut is 'torus'). I have only come across it in an angling context within the *Encyclopedia of Angling* (1994) where it is enigmatically labelled the Policansky knot.

3

4

<139>

G L O S S A R Y

Arbor	The axle, spindle or middle of a reel spool, to which fishing line is attached.
Backing line	Nylon monofilament or braided Dacron loaded onto a fly reel, beneath the fly line, both to fill up the spool and to cope with long runs by fish.
Barrel knot	See **Blood knot.**
Bight	An acute U-shaped bend or partial loop in a monofilament, braid, wire or cable.
Blood knot	Any one of a group of strong and secure barrel-shaped knots, with characteristic wrapping turns, preferred by anglers and climbers (the name being derived from their supposed use by surgeons for tying ligatures and sutures).
Braid	A plaited or interwoven line of greater strength and durability than most monofilaments. The words plait and braid are today virtually synonymous and interchangeable. If there ever was a real difference in meaning, it could be that plaits were flat while braids had a three-dimensional cross-section.
Breaking strength	The load that manufacturers calculate will cause a line to fail, taking no account of any wear and tear, knots, or other weakening factors (see also **Efficiency**).
Butt	The thicker part of a tapering leader, usually monofilament, that is attached to the fly line (see also **Tapered leader**).
Capsize	To become deformed due to incorrect tying, or misuse.
Efficiency	The strength of any knot, expressed as a percentage of the breaking strength of the line in which it is tied.
Elbow	Two crossing points, close together, created by a twisted bight.
End	The working end or free end of a monofilament, braid, wire or cable (see also **Standing end**).
Eye	A small loop.
Fly line	An attachment from fly to leader, of coated nylon, Dacron or PVC.
Flype	British dialect word meaning to turn inside out in a smooth peeling action.
Kink	A very small tightened loop that permanently deforms and weakens a monofilament, braid, wire or cable.
Knot	Angling – the generic term for all accidental or deliberate entanglements or ties, including those joining lines together, forming loops in the ends of lines, and attaching lines to hooks, lures, sinkers and swivels.
Lead (Say 'leed'.)	The direction taken by the working end of any line as it proceeds to form a knot.
Leader	A short length of nylon monofilament, braid or wire attaching a fishing hook, lure or fly to a line, tapered in for fly lines.
Line	Angling – any monofilament or braid, wire or cable, used in a rig assembly; boating – a term for any rope or cord with a specific function (e.g. mooring line, towline).
Loop	A bight twisted to create a crossing point.
Loop knot	A fixed loop, as opposed to a running (sliding) noose (see also **Noose**).
Lure	An artificial bait.

<140>

Monofilament Fishing – pliable and strong nylon fishing line.

Nip The point within a knot where friction is concentrated.

Noose A running (sliding) adjustable loop, as opposed to a fixed loop (see also **Loop knot**).

Nylon The first man-made fibre of merit to be widely marketed. There are two grades: Nylon 66 is extensively used in the UK and USA; Nylon 6 (trade names Perlon and Enkalon) is widely available in Europe and Japan as well as in the UK and USA.

Overhand loop A loop in which the working end goes over the standing part of the line (see also **Underhand loop**).

Part Any section of a knot.

Plait See **Braid**.

Plug An artificial hooked bait resembling a dead fish that can be made to dart and vibrate so as to attract predation.

Polyester A widely used synthetic line, particularly braided (trade names: Dacron and Terylene).

Round turn Describes the way in which a working end completely encircles an eye, ring, monofilament, braid, wire or cable, or another line, and is then brought back alongside its own standing part.

Shock tippet A length of heavier line, knotted to the main line, to absorb the sudden load of a striking fish.

Snell A whipping or binding that secures line to the straight shank of a hook, especially an eyeless (spade-ended) one.

Snood A hook-carrying branch line.

Standing end The unused end of a line, opposite to the working end, and including a reel attachment.

Standing part That part of a line between the working and standing ends.

Strength See **Efficiency** and **Breaking strength**.

Super braids Exceptionally strong, braided lines made from so-called 'miracle fibres' of gel-spun polyethylene or aramid with remarkable strength-to-weight properties.

Tag (or tag end) Angling – the knotted end of a line, particularly the cut and trimmed end that emerges from a tight knot.

Tapered leader A fly leader, commonly 3-4m (9-12ft) long, with a strong 13.6kg (30lb) thick end, tapering down to a weaker 1.8kg (4lb) thin end (see also **Butt** and **Tippet**).

Tippet The thin end or portion of a tapered lead, or the end of a straight light line, to which the fly is tied.

Turn A 360 degree wrap around an eye, ring, line, wire or cable (see also **Round turn**).

Underhand loop A loop in which the working end goes under the standing part of the line (see also **Overhand loop**).

Whipping The generic term for various kinds of binding or wrapping turns (see also **Snell**).

Working end The active end of a line, directly involved in the twisting, interweaving or tucking and tying of a knot.

<141>

BIBLIOGRAPHY

*Asher, Harry, **The Alternative Knot Book**,
  Nautical Books/A. & C. Black London (1989)

Ashley, Clifford W., **The Ashley Book of Knots**,
  Doubleday, Doran & Co. New York (1944)/
  Faber & Faber (1947)

Barnes, Stanley, **Anglers' Knots in Gut and Nylon**,
  Cornish Brothers Ltd., Birmingham(1948)

*Blandford, Percy W., **Practical Knots and Ropework**,
  Tab Books (1980)

Cacutt, Len (editor), **Encyclopedia of Angling**,
  Marshall Cavendish Ltd., London (1985)

Cowburn, Fred, **Angling with 'Luron' 2**, ICI Ltd.,
  London (undated, c1950s)

Davies, W.E., **Fly Dressing and some Tackle Making**,
  Elliot Right Way Books, Kingswood, Surrey (1978)

Day, Cyrus L., **Quipus and Witches' Knots**,
  University of Kansas (1967)

Graumont, Raoul, and Wenstrom, Elmer, **Fisherman's Knots
  and Nets**, Cornell Maritime Press, New York (1948)

Griend, P. van de, and Turner, J.C. (editors), **History and Science
  of Knots**, World Scientific Publishing Co. Pte. Ltd.,
  Singaporre, New Jersey, London, Hong Kong (1996)

Hunter, W.A., **Fisherman's Knots and Wrinkles**,
  A. & C. Black (1927)

Kreh, Lefty, and Sosin, Mark, **Practical Fishing & Boating
  Knots,** A. & C. Black Ltd., London (1972)

Lewis, Derek, **Great Knots & How to Tie Them**,
  Sterling Publishing Co. Inc., New York (1997)

McNally, Bob, **Fishermen's Knots, Fishing Rigs and How to
  Use Them**, McNally Outdoor Productions, Jacksonville,
  Florida ((1993)

Miscellaneous contributors, **Luron for Angling**, ICI Ltd.,
  London (undated, c1950s)

Nilsson, Harry, **The Little Red Fishing Knot Book**, published
  by the author, Canada (1997)

Owen, Peter, **The Pocket Guide to Fishing Knots**,
  Merlin Unwin Books, Ludlow, Shropshire (1998)

Sea Angler magazine, **An Efficient Stop Knot**, (January 1977)

Sosin, Mark and Kreh, Lefty, **Practical Fishing Knots**,
  Lyons & Burford, New York (1991)

Step-by-Step Fishing, Marshall Cavendish Ltd., London (1977)

Trench, Charles Chenevix, **A History of Angling**, Hart-Davis,
  MacGibbon Ltd., London (1974)

Vare, Alan B., **The Hardy Book of Fisherman's Knots**,
  Camden Publishing Co. Ltd., London (1987)

Wilson, Geoff, **Complete Book of Fishing Knots & Rigs**, AFN.,
  Australia (1995)

Yewlett, G., **Catching Coarse Fish**, published by the author,
  Wokingham, Berkshire (1975)

THE INTERNATIONAL GUILD OF KNOT TYERS

The Guild was established in 1982 by 27 individuals and now has a membership approaching 1,000 in countries from Australia to Zimbabwe. It is a UK registered educational charity and anyone interested in knots may join.

Guild members – who include many anglers – are a friendly crowd, novice and expert alike, brought together by their common pursuit of knot tying. Those within travelling distance may enjoy two major weekend meetings held in England each year, with talks, demonstrations and expert tuition freely available, where cordage, ropeworking tools and books (new, second-hand and rare) are also bought, sold or swapped. In areas where many Guild members live, national or regional branches have been formed and these arrange more frequent gatherings and activity programmes.

The thinly scattered worldwide IGKT membership keeps in touch via a members' handbook and a quarterly magazine, *Knotting Matters*, which is full of informed articles, expert tips, letters, editorial comment, news and views about everything imaginable on the knot tying scene. The Guild also sells its own instructional publications and other knotting supplies by mail order.

For further details and an application form, contact:

Nigel Harding (IGKT Hon. Secretary)

3 Walnut Tree Meadow

Stonham Aspal

Stowmarket

Suffolk IP14 6DF

England

Tel: (01449) 711 121

e-mail: igkt@nigelharding.demon.co.uk

Knotting may also be found on the Internet.

<142>

INDEX

<143>

THE TAG END

There are hundreds of good knots that can be used by fishermen.
And many fishermen consider it a measure of angling skill if
they're the master of several dozen . . .
Bob McNally, 1993

It might be thought that knotting is an anachronism, an outmoded practice in the increasingly high-tech tackle-driven pursuit of fishing. Knots could, one might argue, be replaced by patent clips and couplings, universal joints and streamlined joint sleeves. Such items could be manufactured, enabling rigs to be assembled like a toy construction kit. But there is a limit to how much hard-earned cash we should spend on various gadgets, with the energy consumption of scarce planetary resources their production would entail, when a 1-2m (3-6ft) length of line and the right couple of knots will do at least as

well and often better. If a factory-made product fails, perversely when the shops are shut or the user is a long way from civilization, there may be no other option than to discard it. Knots can always be re-tied and re-tried. One knot fits a range of line sizes, is often multi-purpose in its application, and may even incorporate a degree of slide-&-grip shock absorbance. One cannot know too many, as they take up no space in the tackle box, nor do they have to be inspected prior to passing through customs and immigration during foreign travel!

This book has introduced a selection of fishing knots and described certain basic tying methods. There are more fluent individual sleight-of-hand tying techniques that can only be acquired from practised repetition, and innumerable ways in which these knots might be incorporated into fishing rigs. For such advanced knotting know-how, consult any experienced and accomplished angler with time to spare, who is willing to share his or her knowledge in a more practical setting.

2007

<144>